A KID'S GUIDE TO THE **ARMOR OF GOD**

TONY EVANS

HARVEST HOUSE PUBLISHERS
EUGENE, OREGON

Unless otherwise indicated, all Scripture quotations are from the Holy Bible, New International Version®, NIV®. Copyright © 1973, 1978, 1984, 2011 by Biblica, Inc.® Used by permission. All rights reserved worldwide.

Verses marked NASB are taken from the New American Standard Bible®, © 1960, 1962, 1963, 1968, 1971, 1972, 1973, 1975, 1977, 1995 by The Lockman Foundation. Used by permission. (www.Lockman.org)

Design and production by Left Coast Design, Portland, Oregon

Cover illustration © Krieg Barry

HARVEST KIDS is a registered trademark of The Hawkins Children's LLC. Harvest House Publishers, Inc., is the exclusive licensee of the federally registered trademark HARVEST KIDS.

A KID'S GUIDE TO THE ARMOR OF GOD
Copyright © 2015 Tony Evans
Published by Harvest House Publishers
Eugene, Oregon 97408
www.harvesthousepublishers.com

Library of Congress Cataloging-in-Publication Data
    Evans, Tony, 1949- author.
    A kid's guide to the armor of God / Tony Evans.
       pages cm
    Audience: Ages 8-12.
    ISBN 978-0-7369-6056-4 (pbk.)
    ISBN 978-0-7369-6057-1 (eBook)
    1. Spiritual warfare—Juvenile literature. 2. Christian life—Juvenile literature.
    3. Conduct of life—Juvenile literature. I. Title. II. Title: Armor of God.
    BV4509.5.E93 2014
    235'.4—dc23

                                     2014025429

Printed in the United States of America

20 21 / BP-CD / 10 9

Contents

Let's Get Ready!

Did you know that there's an invisible war happening all around you? It's a huge war. It started at the beginning of time—when the world was first created—and it's being fought all throughout the earth. Yet nobody has ever seen it. It's a *spiritual war*.

A spiritual war might sound like it's imaginary—like a made-up war in a book or a movie—but it *is* real. And it affects everyone in the world—even kids like you!

So, what exactly is spiritual warfare? Spiritual warfare is a battle fought between God and Satan that goes on in the invisible, spiritual world—the world you *can't* see—while playing out in the visible, physical world—the world you *can* see—at the same time.

In spiritual warfare God and Satan are battling each other for control of your life. Now, it's important to remember that God is the One who is truly in control. He's already won the battle! But Satan wants to make you think that he's the one in control, so he tries to get to you in any way he can. He likes to play games with people—even kids. He loves to make you feel worried or scared or angry.

Why does Satan do this? Because when you start thinking his way, you stop thinking about God. And that's Satan's main strategy in the spiritual war. The devil wants you to believe that he—not God—is in control. He wants to make your life miserable, and he wants you to think that there's nothing you can do about it.

Don't believe Satan for a second!

When things go wrong in your life, God wants you to turn to Him. He wants to hear your prayers, comfort you, and help you through your troubles. As you turn to Him, you get to know Him better and discover His amazing plan for your life. Satan, however, wants to turn you away from God and keep you from doing what God has planned for you to do. That's the heart of spiritual warfare—Satan trying to tear you away from God.

That's a lot to think about, isn't it? But there's good news! God has already given you the perfect guide to help you understand the spiritual battles you face. This guide is God's Word. His Word tells you exactly what you need to do to win the spiritual war. And in His Word, God reveals that He has already given you six tried-and-tested pieces of armor that will help you win the battle.

In this book we're going to take a look at the six pieces of armor—the belt of truth, the breastplate of righteousness, the shoes of peace, the shield of faith, the helmet of salvation, and the sword of the Spirit—and see how each one helps you fight Satan's sneaky schemes. When Satan tries to get you to worry, think bad thoughts about yourself, or make wrong choices, you can suit up in the armor of God and stand strong.

So, let's get going. It's time to put on God's armor and prepare to win the war!

1
The **Belt** of Truth

Playing at your favorite amusement park! Backpacking in the mountains! Body surfing on the beach!

No matter where you go or what you do, vacations are amazing! You and your family have fun spending time planning the trip, dreaming about the sights you're going to see, the things you're going to do, even the food you're going to eat.

But before you go on your trip, there's something pretty important that you need to do—you need to pack. You can't just show up at the airport or head out to your car with the clothes you have on and expect them to last for the entire vacation. Instead, you fill your suitcase or your duffel bag with all the clothes and belongings you'll need for the entire trip.

You also need to look at the weather forecast to see what kind of clothes you'll need to pack for your vacation. A summer trip to Hawaii is going to call for very different clothes than a fall campout in the mountains. Where you are going will determine what you pack for the trip.

Therefore put on the full armor of God, so that when the day of evil comes, you may be able to stand your ground, and after you have done everything, to stand. Stand firm then, with the belt of truth buckled around your waist, with the breastplate of righteousness in place, and with your feet fitted with the readiness that comes from the gospel of peace. In addition to all this, take up the shield of faith, with which you can extinguish all the flaming arrows of the evil one. Take the helmet of salvation and the sword of the Spirit, which is the word of God (Ephesians 6:13-17).

In the Bible God has given you clear instructions about the specific articles of clothing that you not only need to wear but also need to have packed and ready to put on if you are going to have victory in spiritual warfare. This list of armor can be compared to a travel guide that you read when you're going somewhere new. For example, if you're going to summer camp, the camp brochure often includes a checklist of things to bring—a swimsuit for the pool or lake, long pants and closed-toe shoes for horseback riding, and a warm jacket for chilly nights around the campfire.

Where is your favorite place to go on vacation?

_____

_____

What kind of clothes do you pack when you go there?

_____

_____

Why is it so important that you know what to wear? *Because you are in a battle*. And the battle isn't against flesh and blood. It isn't against other people. The root of the battle lies in the spiritual world, so you need a spiritual wardrobe to fight this battle.

If you go through life as a follower of Christ, but you're dressed all wrong for a spiritual battle, you'll never be able to win the battle and live the amazing life God designed you to live. You'll be missing out on the best experience ever!

TIED TO A LEASH

Have you ever been to an amusement park or a public place where there are a lot of children? Occasionally, when I go to one of these places, I'll see a mother or a father with a leash around his or her wrist. Naturally my mind thinks that the leash is going to be attached to a dog. But then I look and notice that the leash is actually attached to a child! Apparently some children need more than their parent's words to keep them nearby.

Unfortunately the same is true for many Christians as well! God has already told you in His Word how to find your greatest source of strength—it's your closeness to Him. It is in this location—right next to Christ—that you are supposed to "stand firm." You're supposed to live your life right beside Jesus, not wandering away like the child at the amusement park.

Time to Get Dressed!

Now, let's get to our first article of clothing—the belt of truth.

A belt? Do people even wear belts anymore? you might think. Sure they do! And while you probably don't wear belts with most of your outfits, a belt can actually be quite useful.

Ephesians 6:14 says, "Stand firm then, with the belt of truth buckled around your waist..." In Bible times Roman soldiers always wore belts. In fact, a Roman soldier's belt was a very useful tool. First of all, it was a place where he could hang some of his other armor, like his sword or his dagger. If you've ever watched a movie that takes place in Roman times, you've seen the men dressed in long robes, which were called tunics. (Aren't you glad *that* fashion trend is over?) When the soldier was ready to head into battle, he could reach down and pick up the part of his tunic that was hanging down near his feet and tuck it into the belt. Now he could move his feet freely and head into the action! See how useful that belt was?

So, what can a belt do for *you*? One thing a belt can do is hold up your pants or skirt. The second thing it can do is keep your shirt tucked in (like when you're dressing up for something). A belt can also make a fashion statement, but most importantly a belt holds together whatever else you're wearing.

A belt is designed to hold your outfit together by keeping your items of clothing in their proper order—pants held up and shirt tucked in. The belt of truth holds the rest of your *spiritual* armor together.

Satan, however, wants to mess up your outfit. He wants

to unbuckle your belt of truth so that your pants fall down and your shirt comes untucked. Of course he doesn't *literally* want your clothing all messed up. He wants to create chaos and disorder in your life so that you lose your focus on God and worry about the things going on all around you.

The enemy does this because he's all about lying. Jesus is all about truth. Jesus said in John 8:32, "Then you will know the truth, and the truth will set you free."

Here's an important thing to remember: Just reading the truth or seeing the truth doesn't set you free. Rather, it is the truth that you "know" that will set you free.

So what is truth? Truth, at its core, is God's view of a matter. And truth is so powerful that it changes lives both right at this moment and *also* for all eternity. The presence of God's truth brings understanding and victory, but the absence of it brings confusion and defeat. Truth is powerful, isn't it?

THREE THINGS ABOUT TRUTH

1. Though truth is made up of information and facts, it also includes God's original intent—or purpose. This makes it the absolute standard by which we can measure everything else.

   Let me tell a story to help explain this to you. A man went fishing one day and brought home 20 catfish. He told his wife, "Honey, I caught 20 catfish today." That was a fact. He had brought home the 20 catfish he'd caught.

His wife, however, knew he wasn't a very good fisherman, so she asked him, "How did you catch 20 catfish?"

He answered, "Well, I went to the fish market and asked the guy to toss me 20 catfish, and I caught them all!"

This man gave his wife the facts, but he didn't give her the truth. In fact he hid the facts in his "truth." Truth always includes more than facts. It includes the goal—or purpose—behind the facts.

2. Truth has already been predetermined—or decided in advance—by God. Truth doesn't change with the latest fashion or fad. Truth is reality in its original form.

One plus one equals two. One plus one has always equaled two. It will always be so. Even when I don't feel like one plus one should equal two, and I really feel like I want it to equal three, one plus one will still equal two. Even if I hope, believe, and claim that one plus one should equal three, one plus one will never equal three because you can't change the laws of mathematics!

Truth is a powerful reality predetermined by God. And your thoughts and actions need to line up with God's truth.

3. What is true of you on the inside needs to be true of you on the outside. Your actions, decisions, conversations, and choices need to reflect what's

inside of you. Being honest with who you are and figuring out why you do the things that you do—why you choose certain friends, how you react when something goes wrong, what you decide to spend your time on—is something you need to do when you buckle on the belt of truth.

God knows when you're faking it. After all, He already knows everything about you. He knows when you're hiding something from Him. You can't shock God. You can't surprise God. He already knows it all.

God knows the past, present, and future of everything—your thoughts, your actions, and even what you want to do that you don't do. When you get real with God, you will find it much easier to get real with yourself.

Figuring Out the Truth

Here's one question I want you to ask yourself about truth: How will you figure out what is true?

How do you know if something is true?

_____

_____

Do your feelings tell you what is true? Feelings change—sometimes you're up, sometimes you're down, sometimes you're happy, and sometimes you're sad.

What if I told you I was going to give you a million dollars? Your feelings might fly high! You'll be rich! You'll be able to buy anything you want! But then what if I told you that the million dollars was in play money? You'd probably scream or get pretty upset with me!

You need to understand your feelings because they are real, but you should never use them as your main guide to figuring out the truth.

What about using your intelligence to figure out what's true? I know that you're smart, but do you know absolutely *everything*? Of course not! Nobody does (except God!). Have you ever learned something and then found out some new information that changed your opinion? God is the only one who has *all* the information.

What about using your morals—your sense of right and wrong—to figure out the truth? You might think you have a pretty good sense of right and wrong, but even that can change with your feelings, new information, the influence of other people, and just general growing up.

So what will you choose to figure out if something is true? Will you use your feelings (which are constantly changing), your intelligence (which is limited—you don't know it all), or your sense of right and wrong (which you can never quite figure out on this earth)? Or will you choose God to show you the truth?

Only God is the creator of truth. Knowing Him and His Word is the only way to know how to use the belt of truth because only God can say what is entirely true.

What Is Real?

Have you ever been to an amusement park and seen the mirrors that make you look fat, tall, short, or skinny? The mirrors *distort*—or change—your real image. Did you know that your soul has become distorted like these mirrors? It's all because of sin. Sin has gotten into your soul and twisted it so it no longer looks how it was created to look.

A person looking into a carnival mirror couldn't accurately describe the true person who is being reflected in the mirror. Neither can you accurately say what truth is when you look through the distorted mirror of your soul. The soul within you—how you see a matter—needs to be restored. You do this by exchanging your thoughts for God's truth.

How can you swap out your thoughts (which by now you know you can't always trust or rely upon) for God's truth? You do this by asking for help from the third person of the Trinity—the Holy Spirit. (The other two are God the Father and Jesus, who is God the Son.) First Corinthians 2:10 says, "The Spirit searches all things, even the deep things of God." This means that part of the Holy Spirit's work is to continually—which means all the time—examine everything. Even all things about God!

Isn't that terrific? The Holy Spirit—who was sent by God to this earth to be your helper—can give you the ability to know God. By knowing God, you receive the truth that lets you walk in victory in your daily life—on your very best day *and* on your very worst day!

The belt of truth is hanging in your closet ready to go! Satan, though, doesn't want you to wear it. In fact he'll do anything to keep you from putting it on. "God's truth doesn't look good on you," he might whisper. "That belt of truth doesn't fit you. It's not your style."

His wrong thoughts—another name for them is *lies*—pop into your mind until you're not sure who's right, who's wrong, and what in the world you should believe.

Wrong thoughts aren't just whispered directly into your mind by Satan. Sure, they can show up that way, but the enemy can also get to you in other ways. It might be something as harmless as a teacher giving an opinion about what you should do or think. It could be what your friends or the media—in the form of popular songs, movies, or TV shows—are persuading you to do or believe. It could even be what you read in a hard-to-put-down novel that changes your way of thinking and pulls you away from God's truth.

What are some ways that wrong thoughts could be put into your mind?

_____

_____

Here's another *really* important thing to remember: Satan doesn't care if you mix some of God's truth in with the rest of the "truth" you've gathered from all of your other sources (like friends, books, and movies) because he knows that if he can twist what you believe to be true, that's enough to prevent you from putting on the belt of truth and really knowing God.

DANGEROUS LASAGNA AHEAD!

One day a restaurant chef prepared a pan of lasagna. He sliced up the tomatoes, boiled the noodles, fried the meat, and added some chopped onions and garlic along with cheese and sauce.

Then just as he was about to put the pan in the oven, he sprinkled poison all over the top.

Would you eat that lasagna? No way! But that's what Satan does to strip you of the belt of truth. He says, "Go to church. Read your Bible. Memorize your verses. But at the end of the day, sprinkle in a little bit about what the world says, what your teachers say, how your friends think, what television or movies show, or whatever else you feel, desire, or want to believe." Satan knows that when you've done that, you've taken off the belt of truth. And do you know something crazy? Satan didn't have to take it off for you. You took it off all by yourself!

Avoid the dangerous lasagna! Stick to a dish that you know all the ingredients. Eat at a restaurant where the chef tells the truth!

Before we move on to the next article of clothing, let's review the three principles of truth. First, truth is made up of information and facts, but it also includes God's original intent, which makes it the absolute standard by which you can measure everything else. Second, truth has already been predetermined—decided ahead of time—by God. And third, what is true of you on the inside needs to be true of you on the outside.

When you put on the belt of truth and align your mind, your heart, and your emotions with God's truth, He will then give you all the power you need to fight your spiritual battles. And you'll be well on your way to experiencing victory over anything or anyone who seeks to overcome or defeat you.

Why is the belt of truth the first piece of armor you need to put on?

_____

_____

How is the world's truth different from God's truth? How can you learn to measure things by God's truth?

_____

_____

What are some good ways to discover God's truth?

_____

_____

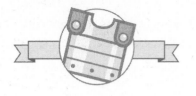

2

The **Breastplate** of Righteousness

I f you're a Christian—a person who has accepted Christ as his or her Savior—Satan can't take away your salvation, but he *can* ruin your life—if you let him. He fights really hard to do this! He wages an all-out war to keep you from experiencing all the amazing things God has planned for you right now and in the future.

One way Satan tries to do this is by turning your attention away from the spiritual realm and onto the physical realm. Instead of focusing on talking to God through prayer, reading what He says in the Bible, and listening to His voice of truth, Satan wants you to focus on the things of this world—what you can see, taste, touch, smell, or hear. He doesn't want you to think about him or his demons either! He'd rather get to you in sneaky ways.

Now, your five senses—sight, taste, touch, smell, and sound—are important, but if you choose to depend only upon your five senses to make choices in life, you're headed for trouble. Skateboarding without a helmet and pads might look like fun, but doing it in reality is quite danger-ous. Cotton candy might taste terrific, but eating a diet of only cotton candy would be very bad for your health. A pop-ular song might have a great tune, but listening to the song's bad words and negative message over and over is terrible for your mind.

Satan will use as much as he can in the physical world—the world of the five senses—to keep you down.

Something That Nobody Can Take Away

So far we've looked at the first piece of God's armor—the belt of truth. After the belt of truth, God gives us the next item in our wardrobe—the breastplate of righteous-ness. Ephesians 6:14 says, "Stand firm then, with the belt of truth buckled around your waist, with the breastplate of righteousness in place..."

Righteousness is a pretty long word. What does it mean? It's actually quite simple. Righteousness simply means being or doing what is right. (You knew it had something to do with the word *right*, didn't you?)

The belt of truth comes first because there can't be righ-teousness without truth. In order to know that something is *right*, you need to know that it is *true*.

There are two sides to righteousness—the *being* side and the *doing* side. Righteousness is assigned—or given—to everyone who trusts in Jesus Christ for the forgiveness of their sins. This means that God has done even more than forgive your sins through Jesus Christ. He has also put righteousness into your account, like birthday money your grandparents put in your bank account. The righteousness now belongs to you. Nobody can take it away from you. Even

Satan can't take it away. Ever! Once you are saved, Satan can do nothing to change your righteous standing before God.

Of course you know that Satan is going to try to do *something* to keep you from putting on the breastplate of righteousness! He knows he can't take away your righteous standing before God, so he looks for a way to break your fellowship with God. He's like someone who is doing everything he can to break up the terrific friendship between you and your best friend. (Well, that's exactly what *is* happening. God is your best friend!)

Nobody's Perfect!

Nobody's perfect. I'm sure you've heard that saying before. There isn't a person on this planet who can live his or her life without sinning. And even if it doesn't look like someone is sinning, I can assure you that he or she *is* sinning in one way or another.

If you want to read a book, you can choose from several different formats. You can read a book on a tablet like an iPad or a Kindle. You can listen to an audiobook, or you can read an old-fashioned, turn-the-pages book. Like a book, sin comes in a variety of formats. There are *overt* sins, which are done outwardly through our actions, like cheating or bullying. There are also *covert* sins, which take place in our minds, hearts, and emotions. This would include things like being super jealous of someone else or even having feelings of hatred toward another person. Beyond that there are sins of *commission*—doing things the Bible says we should not do—and sins of *omission*—not doing things the Bible says we ought to do.

Do you remember how we talked about truth being not

only information and facts but also the purpose behind that information and those facts? Like truth, righteousness is about more than doing the right thing. Righteousness includes the motivation behind doing the right things and not doing the wrong things. You could do the right thing (being really nice and helpful to your parents) but mess it up with the wrong motivation (acting that way in order to get out of a punishment you deserved *or* in order to get a reward).

> Can you think of a time when you did the right thing for the wrong reason?

> _____

> _____

STANDING UP ON THE INSIDE

A young boy was told by his teacher to sit down. He didn't want to sit down, but he knew he would get in trouble if he didn't. So he sat down. Yet in his heart he said, *I'm sitting down on the outside, but I'm standing up on the inside.* Unlike the boy's teacher, who can't see his heart, God sees deep within you and measures the motivation of all that you do or don't do.

Digging for Dirty Clothes

You might be surprised if you were able to see sin the way God sees it. First John 3:15 says, "Anyone who hates a brother or sister is a murderer." That's pretty intense! But sin is sin—murder is sin, and hating someone is also sin. Satan wants you to live a life of sin—any kind of sin—because sin pulls you away from God.

The good news is that when you confess your sin—when you tell God what you've done wrong and say you're sorry for it—He will remove the stain of that sin from you. "If we confess our sins, he is faithful and just and will forgive us our sins and purify us from all unrighteousness" (1 John 1:9).

Have you ever pulled your favorite T-shirt or pair of shorts out of the dirty clothes basket? Maybe you just wore the shirt yesterday and spilled food on it, or you got the shorts muddy playing soccer with your friends. You *really* want to wear them again, so you sneak them out of the dirty clothes basket and hope that nobody notices the smell or the stain.

Believe it or not, something like that happened in the Bible! Zechariah 3 tells about a preacher named Joshua who came before the Lord with dirty clothes on. Joshua came before God in his unrighteousness. He didn't do what many of us try to do and hide his dirty clothes from God. He also didn't try to persuade God to believe that his clothes really weren't as dirty as they appeared. (Do these tricks sound familiar to you?) He just stood before God in his unrighteousness, wearing the dirty clothes and not trying to hide anything.

> Then he showed me Joshua the high priest standing before the angel of the LORD, and Satan standing at his right side to accuse him. The LORD said to Satan, "The LORD rebuke you, Satan! The LORD, who has chosen Jerusalem, rebuke you! Is

not this man a burning stick snatched from the fire?" Now Joshua was dressed in filthy clothes as he stood before the angel. The angel said to those who were standing before him, "Take off his filthy clothes." Then he said to Joshua, "See, I have taken away your sin, and I will put fine garments on you." Then I said, "Put a clean turban on his head." So they put a clean turban on his head and clothed him, while the angel of the LORD stood by (Zechariah 3:1-5).

God responded to Joshua's dirty clothes and Satan's accusation by removing Joshua's sinfulness—his dirty clothes—and covering him instead with fine garments—clothes designed especially for him for a unique and special purpose. Joshua hadn't done anything to deserve the fine garments. God gave them to Joshua out of His mercy.

Do you know what Satan's number-one hobby is? His all-time favorite thing to do is accusing you and me of all the wrong things we have ever done or thought. He likes to remind us about all the times we've talked back to our parents or made our little brother cry. He wants us to focus on the lies we've told and the mean words we've said to our friends. The enemy wants us to keep digging that soiled shirt out of the dirty clothes, so he can remind us just how filthy we are.

Instead of dwelling on the dirt, we need to come clean with God. How do we do this? We confess our sins to God. When we pray we too often focus on asking God to bless us, take care of us, and protect us. Now, there's nothing wrong with asking for help when we pray. God wants to help us! But don't forget the confession part of praying. When we confess our sins to God and receive His forgiveness, He puts us back into our position of righteousness as a child of God. He adjusts the breastplate of righteousness in our spiritual armor so that we can have victory.

What is something that you can confess to God right now?

_____

_____

How do you feel after telling God about this?

_____

_____

TAKE OUT THE TRASH

Taking out the trash—not exactly my favorite chore! Trash is messy. And it smells! But it needs to be done. Having trash hanging around in your house isn't the best idea. Trash or food left on the counters or on the floor is the perfect environment for pests—like ants or even roaches—to come and live in. It's like putting down a welcome mat for these pesky critters!

Guess what happens next? The ants or roaches will invite their cousins and make themselves at home in your trash. These pests are like demons who make themselves at home in the trash that is sin. They love hanging out where sin is being committed, and they're very content sticking around where sin has not been confessed, so confess that sin and take out the trash!

Get Rid of the Mess!

Have you ever been asked to clean your room but instead decided to just move things around so your room *looks* clean? Instead of separating the clean clothes from the dirty ones, you just shove the whole pile back in your drawer. Instead of sorting through the school papers and books you have scattered across the floor, you cram everything back into your backpack. Instead of picking up the toys and games that cover your carpet and putting them back where they belong, you kick the whole mess under your bed. Does your room look clean? Maybe. But it wouldn't take much detective work to discover the hidden mess.

It's the same way with sin. Instead of confessing and removing the sin and unrighteousness from our lives, we often end up settling for trash management. We want to move stuff here, adjust things there, and hide stuff so we don't appear to have much trash. Your life—like your room—might look clean, but the mess is still there because you haven't taken the time to deal with the actual items that are making up the mess. Can you see the mess? Not right away. Is it still there? You bet!

Not wearing the breastplate of righteousness is like refusing to really clean up your room. Two things happen in spiritual warfare when you don't wear the breastplate of righteousness. First, an invitation is sent out to allow demons to hang out in the messy room that is your life. Second, God's power can't really move within and through you because there is a break in your fellowship with God. God does not hang out in a messy room, even if the mess is hidden. God does not abide with darkness.

Protect Your Heart

An important thing to know about the breastplate of righteousness is what it is designed to protect—the heart.

Why is it so important to protect your heart? Because your heart is the thing that makes the rest of you—your eyes and ears, lungs and legs, and mouth and muscles—work. If the heart stops, everything else stops. The heart is incredibly important!

> Above all else, guard your heart, for everything
> you do flows from it (Proverbs 4:23).

The heart is a physical pump that controls the flow of blood throughout your body. Your spiritual heart—your essence, your core, and the thing that makes you *you*—is the pump that God uses to fill you with new life. Do you remember that once you trust Christ for your salvation, you were made new with His righteousness? Second Corinthians 5:17 says, "Therefore, if anyone is in Christ, the new creation has come: The old has gone, the new is here!"

Now, you're made up of three distinct parts: body, soul, and spirit. Sometimes we talk as if our soul is the part that is made new at salvation. We say things like, "Jesus saved my soul," but the thing that was immediately made new when we became Christians was our spirit. Your soul is in the process of being *sanctified*—being made more holy, more dedicated to God—and made new over time. That's why you can be a Christian and still have problems with getting mad or feeling bad about yourself. Your soul—your mind, will, and emotions—is still not perfect, and it's the thing that's telling your body what to do.

The work of the new spirit within you is to pump life into the soul so that eventually your new spirit has the most say in what you feel, think, and do. You can make changes on the outside—going to church more, putting more money on the offering plate, singing louder in Sunday school—but the real victory comes on the inside when the new spirit within you pumps God's truth into the different areas of your life.

Basically your soul can't fix your soul. Your soul can't be righteous on its own. As you allow the new life of the Spirit to change your soul, you will find true and lasting victory. You'll be a proud wearer of the breastplate of righteousness.

One of the reasons you might not be experiencing victory in spiritual warfare is that you're trying to force a man-made breastplate of righteousness onto yourself instead of accepting God's truth as the standard of righteousness He wants you to wear. It's like trying to force an infant-sized bike helmet onto an adult's head or trying to stuff your feet into sneakers that are three sizes too small. Try as you might, it's never going to work!

You Are What You Eat

I'm sure you've heard the saying, "You are what you eat." And you know what it means. Good food—protein, fruits, and veggies—builds your body up and makes you strong and healthy. Junky food—candy, chips, and soda—doesn't allow your body to function at its best and—if you eat *too* much junk food—can make you sick.

Did you know that the Bible is to the spirit what food is to the body? As the Word of God feeds your spirit and begins to influence your soul, your actions will begin to naturally reflect God's viewpoint on a matter. They won't just be reactions that you do for a time based on something you read or heard. Your life will completely change as it becomes influenced by the Holy Spirit's presence of truth and righteousness within you.

Eating a few grapes and a forkful of salad isn't going to instantly make you a healthier person. It takes meal after meal of eating right to get the benefits of a wholesome diet. Likewise, feeding the righteousness planted within you will take more than a minute. You need to read God's Word—the Bible—and chew on what He says. You need to think about what God is saying to you over and over and over again. Let God's Word—and His righteousness—become as real to you in your thoughts as whatever you see all around you.

What are some good things to eat that will help your body grow strong?

_____

_____

What are some good things to do that will help feed the righteousness within you?

_____

_____

Not to Worry!

Worrying about something—a test, a friendship, a family problem—can actually make the thing that you're worrying about seem worse over time. Thinking about God's righteousness and His promises, however, will make them more real—and better—to you. Memorize verses and then meditate on those verses all the time—in the shower, during your walk or ride to school, and while you're brushing your teeth. It might sound a little silly, but it works! God's Word will fill your heart and become your breastplate of righteousness.

When truth flows freely from your spirit, it releases righteousness into your soul. As the soul breathes in the righteousness being released into it, it then tells the body, "You have to walk differently. You have to think differently. You have to talk differently. You have to dress differently. You have to choose your friends differently. You have to spend your time differently. You have to live differently. Because you *are* different." Yes, you *are* different—a good kind of different!

The breastplate of righteousness has been deposited within you. It's your job to feed it and nourish it with the truth of God so that it expands to surround you with the protection you need.

If I told you that I had buried ten million dollars in your backyard, you would put this book down right now and make every effort to find a shovel and get to your backyard. You would leave wherever you are and quickly go tear up your yard. You would dig as deep as you needed to dig because the thing you were digging for would have life-impacting value. That ten million dollars would be worth all the effort required to find it.

When you got saved, God deposited deep down within

you all of the righteousness that belongs to Jesus Christ. But you can't benefit from it unless you're willing to dig down deep with the shovel of truth so that God will release a brand-new you surrounded by the secure protection of a breastplate of His righteousness.

When you wear the breastplate of righteousness, you walk securely in the righteousness God has assigned to you as one of His beloved children. When you wear the breastplate of righteousness, God dresses you in sparkling new clothes, and you have no need to dig your filthy ones out of the dirty clothes. When you wear the breastplate of righteousness, you feed your spirit with the Word of God so that the Holy Spirit will produce the natural outgrowth of right living from within you.

What are you waiting for? Strap on that breastplate of righteousness and get ready for the next piece of armor—one that is going to take you places!

LET'S TALK ABOUT IT

What does it mean to be righteous? What does it mean to live righteously?

_____

_____

_____

_____

Sometimes we can really make a mess of our lives! How can God help us clean up the messes we make?

_____

_____

Why is it so important to protect your heart? How does wearing the breastplate of righteousness help you do this?

_____

_____

3

The **Shoes** of Peace

ow many pairs of shoes do you own? You probably have a pair of everyday sneakers—Nikes or Adidas or whatever your favorite brand is. I'm guessing that you have a pair or two of flip-flops, boots for the rain, nice shoes for church or special occasions, and shoes specific to an activity that you do—football cleats, tap shoes, or basketball high-tops.

Whether they're simply the latest trend, the most scientifically proven athletic shoe, or an expensive name brand, shoes play an important part in our lives. They can be symbols of something more than they actually are, as we've seen with Dorothy's ruby slippers in *The Wizard of Oz* or Cinderella's glass one. Shoes are even mentioned in the Bible! When God talked to Moses in the desert and spoke with Joshua at the border of the promised land, He told them to remove their shoes.

What kind of shoes are in your closet?

_____

_____

Not surprisingly, then, the next piece of armor you need for experiencing victory in spiritual warfare is something you put on your feet. After all, you can tell a lot about a person by their shoes!

Get the Right Fit

Ephesians 6:15 says that putting on the full armor of God includes having your feet "fitted with the readiness that comes from the gospel of peace." So not only do you need to wear the belt of truth and the breastplate of righteousness, you also need to put on the right shoes.

Have you ever seen a picture of a Roman soldier's sandals? They're those leather, heavy-soled, combo military boots/sandals. To make the shoes super durable and stable, nails—called hobnails—were firmly placed directly through the soles. Like cleats that football and soccer players wear today, the hobnails gave the solider traction so that he wouldn't slip or slide. He was able to stand steady on his feet, move around easier, and wasn't as likely to be knocked down when he was wearing these shoes.

These are the kind of shoes you want to have as your "peace shoes." *Wait a minute!* you might think. *How can a soldier's war shoes be peace shoes?* Great question! Remember that you're in a battle—a spiritual battle. You need to be in a position where you stand firm and can't easily be knocked down when Satan comes along. You need shoes that dig deep into the solid ground beneath you. You need those hobnailed, military boot/sandal things on your feet!

Even if you've never been knocked down physically, you know what it's like to be knocked down on the inside. When your parents fight with each other, you feel knocked down. When other kids ignore you, you feel knocked down. When you want that part in the play or spot on the team and you don't get it, you feel knocked down.

But it doesn't have to be that way! You don't have to slide or move with every tough situation. Putting on the shoes of peace creates a stability that even Satan can't knock over!

What things in life knock you down?

_____

_____

The Gospel of Peace

The goal of Satan and his demons in spiritual warfare is to make you feel like a loser. Now remember—God's side has already won! But Satan likes to make you forget that. The enemy knows he can't take away your salvation, so he tries to make you a miserable Christian. And if he's successful, you won't be able to experience all the terrific things God has in store for you. You'll miss discovering His purpose for your life, you'll be blind to His blessings in your life, and you won't be able to grow in your relationship with Him.

When you put on your peace shoes, you'll be ready to deal with whatever comes your way. But what is this "gospel of peace" that you're supposed to wear on your feet?

It seems like today we see the word *peace* all over the

place. The popular peace symbol decorates jewelry, bumper stickers, T-shirts, and notebooks. But peace is so much more than a word or a symbol. Peace means different things to different people. In a part of the world where there is a lot of fighting, like the Middle East, it can mean the absence of war. To a busy teacher with an active class of students, it can mean the break when the kids are at recess. To brothers and sisters who are arguing, peace is the time when everyone stops yelling at each other and starts playing together.

The concept of peace is pretty popular in our culture, but you need to understand the concept of God's peace if you're going to put on the third piece of armor—the shoes of peace.

In the Bible peace means completeness, wholeness, and an inner resting of the soul that never changes despite what else is going on. A person who is at peace is someone who is calm, untroubled, and at rest within. A person *not* at peace, of course, is filled with inner chaos, anxiety, and worry.

What do *you* imagine when you think of peace? You might picture a tropical beach with bright blue-green water and waves crashing gently onto a sparkly, sandy shore. Or you might imagine being out in a canoe on a clear-as-glass mountain lake. Perhaps your ideal image of peace is your bedroom—perfectly clean and organized!

What does peace look like to you?

_____

_____

Did you know that you can have peace in the middle of a storm on the beach with the waves crashing all around you?

Peace on a choppy lake as you struggle to paddle your canoe to shore? Peace in the middle of a messy room?

Thunder and lightning might be chasing each other all around you. The wind could be blowing unhappy things into your life. Nothing looks right. Nothing looks promising. Everything's a mess. Did you know that it's in these exact moments when true peace wins the battle? That's because even though you are experiencing chaos on the outside, God's peace on the inside can totally calm your mind.

In fact the Bible says that the peace of God is so completely opposite of the natural way we respond to life's problems that we often can't understand it! Philippians 4:7 says, "And the peace of God, which transcends all understanding, will guard your hearts and your minds in Christ Jesus." Peace protects you!

God gives you a peace that is far beyond what you can understand. How can you feel safe when lightning is striking all around you? How can you feel calm when waves are crashing over your boat? How can you feel unworried when you're frantically searching for your overdue library book in your messy room? You accept God's peace. When you receive and walk in His peace, your heart and mind are settled as you rely on Him. God's peace is so powerful that we're told to let it control us. The Bible instructs us to let God's peace call the shots, make the decisions, and rule our emotions.

PEACE iS YOUR UMPiRE

Colossians 3:15 says, "Let the peace of Christ rule in your hearts." The Greek word used for the word *rule* in this verse means the same thing as "to umpire." Peace is to be our umpire. What is the main job of a baseball umpire? The umpire has the final say in the way things are. If he calls a pitch a ball, it's a ball. If he calls a runner out, the runner's out. The game is centered on what the umpire calls. His word is the rule. Likewise the peace of Christ is to make the call in your life.

This or That

Even at your age, you have a lot of choices to make in life. Should you play soccer or run on the track team? Should you go to summer camp with your best friend or go with a group of new friends? Should you keep saving your money or spend it on that new game? Putting on the shoes of peace can help you make good choices. God says that when you allow His peace to rule your life, He will call the shots. When you're worrying about what you're supposed to do, He will calm your heart and your mind by giving you peace.

What are some choices you need to make?

_____

_____

How can God help you with these choices?

_____

_____

WHEN YOU JUST DON'T KNOW

Have you ever been in a situation where doing something makes sense—and you can't really see anything wrong with it—but inside you're thinking, *I just don't feel right about this. I don't really have any peace about what I'm doing.* Maybe it's hanging out with a person you just met or spending the night at a friend's house—but you don't really know her parents.

In a situation like that and when the feeling of peace is not there, you should wait to make your decision. If the peace of Christ is ruling in your life, that automatically means that the peace of Christ is present. You can feel it. You just know inside. When the peace of Christ isn't present, something else is in charge. That something could be worry. Or anxiety. Or fear. Whatever it is, if there's no inner peace ruling your heart and your mind, you've taken off the peace shoes God made especially for you.

When you just don't know, it's best to pray about your situation and talk to a trusted adult—a parent, grandparent, teacher, or youth leader—about your decision. God will let you know when you just don't know.

Permanent Peace!

Jesus provided a powerful example of peace in the midst of chaos on the night He was to be crucified. Talk about a non-peaceful situation! He was facing the scariest thing you could imagine. He said, "Peace I leave with you; my peace I give you. I do not give to you as the world gives. Do not let your hearts be troubled and do not be afraid" (John 14:27).

What Jesus shows us through these words—and His actions—is that His peace is different from the world's peace. The world might offer you peace in being the star athlete, peace in popularity, peace in a pair of designer jeans, and peace in an iPad. The world serves up peace in many different ways. The problem with the world's peace is that it lasts only as long as the thing itself. Somebody new moves to town and takes your place as the star athlete. You lose your standing in the popular crowd. The designer jeans rip. You drop the iPad—and it breaks. The *thing* that brings you peace ends, and so does the peace.

But the peace that God gives produces rest on the inside. It *remains*. No matter what's going on around you—no matter how awful it seems—you can still have peace. You can handle it. You may not like it, but you can handle it. Jesus says *that* kind of peace is the kind of peace He wants you to have.

> I told you these things, so that in me you may have peace. In this world you will have trouble. But take heart! I have overcome the world (John 16:33).

Putting on Your Peace Shoes

This brings us to an important question: How do you cover your feet with peace? The secret is in the gospel. We have been instructed to put on "the preparation of the gospel of peace." Did you know that *gospel* means *good news*? Yes, you are supposed to put on the good news of peace—news that's so good that it seems too good to be true! To most people, the gift of salvation—God's free gift of salvation and forgiveness of our sins for all who believe in Him—seems too good to be true. But it is true!

At salvation God gave you a new nature. And that new nature is your spirit. The spirit contains all of God's power, presence, joy, peace, righteousness, holiness, and much more. Everything that God has in store for you is already there in that new spirit within you, and it is perfect. Your new spirit is the only place that Satan does not have access to. The problem, though, is that your perfect spirit is making its home within your imperfect soul.

Remember, your soul—like that amusement park mirror we talked about earlier—has become distorted through the consequences of your own sin and also the effect that other people's sin has had on you. Your soul has been affected by what other kids have said and done to you. It's been affected by books, movies, and television. It's been affected by the things you've learned in school.

Your soul—your mind, will, and emotions—is affected by so many different and changing things that you can find yourself acting one way one week and another way another week. Your mood can be happy one day and sad the next because your soul—which is not perfect—is telling your body what to do and how to feel.

Have you noticed that when you get worried about something, your body reacts in a certain way? You might start tapping your feet or drumming your fingers when you get nervous. Or you might stutter or not be able to think of the right words to say. You can even start to have trouble breathing when you're scared.

How do you react when you get worried about something?

_____

_____

Those kinds of physical reactions are exactly what Satan wants in spiritual warfare. The enemy wants you to take off your peace shoes and lose your peace. When you lose your peace, you don't sleep well anymore. You stop thinking clearly. You panic about a test, even though you studied for it. You say things you regret—to your parents, to your friends, to your brother or sister. You do things you know you shouldn't. You become someone you don't even recognize at times.

Our bodies do wrong things because they're following the direction of our distorted souls. Here's something really important to realize: *You can't fix you.* At the most, all you can try to do is control you. So you need to allow God to step in and help with the rest!

Here's how God works: He works from the spirit first, then the soul, and finally the body. So if you want your body to do the right thing, you begin by getting your soul to do the right thing. And if you want your soul to do the right thing, you need to feed and nourish your spirit.

That's a lot to think about, but there's one main thing to remember: *God is the only One who can give you peace, and He starts the process right inside your spirit.* It's terrific to talk to a parent or a Sunday school teacher or a small group leader about your spirit and your soul. Those people can give you great guidance and explain a lot of hard-to-understand ideas, but remember that God is the One who gives you peace. You can always talk to Him, even in a simple prayer like, "God, please give me Your peace." And He will answer!

So how does it work? How does God give you His peace? The Holy Spirit releases the truths, the reality, and the presence of God into your human spirit. Your spirit then delivers it to your soul. Now in order for the soul to grab onto and receive the things of the spirit, it must agree with the spirit. But that doesn't always happen! Remember our souls are distorted—they're far from perfect—so the spirit isn't free to release its power into us. So you need to replace the distortions within you with God's truth. The truth is the only thing that the spirit and the soul can agree upon.

GOD'S PERFECT PEACE

"Family meeting," says your mom. "Meet in the living room in five minutes."

Uh-oh, you think. *This can't be good.*

And you're right. The reason for the family meeting? Your dad lost his job. Money has been tight anyway. Your family already buys clothes at the thrift shop (which is kind of fun, actually) and can't afford to go out to eat (but that's okay because Mom and Dad are both terrific cooks— and you're learning to cook too!).

Now, though, you're worried. Where will your family get money for food? Will you be able to keep taking gymnastics lessons? Are you going to be able to keep your house? What's going to happen?

The truth of God says, "My God will meet all your needs." But the facts are that your family is in trouble. What are you going to believe? The facts that you see—your dad losing his job and money already tight to begin with—or the truth that God will provide for your family's every need?

This is the perfect time to put on your peace shoes and align your soul under the rule of your spirit. When you choose to do that, God will release peace into your life because the peace of Christ is now ruling your thoughts and actions. When worry creeps back in, you remind it that it's lying to you, because God has promised that He will provide.

Thank You Very Much!

Philippians 4:6-7 says, "Do not be anxious about anything, but in every situation, by prayer and petition, with thanksgiving, present your requests to God. And the peace of God, which transcends all understanding, will guard your hearts and your minds in Christ Jesus."

Why does the Bible tell us to go to God with thanksgiving? Think of an acorn. A small, seemingly insignificant acorn (which is a tree seed) has everything within it to become a towering oak tree. All it needs is nourishment—sunlight, water, air—and then it will grow.

The acorn is like your spirit. You don't have to add anything to it. God has already put in your spirit everything it will ever need. Now, this is where the going to God with thanksgiving comes in. When you have problems or needs of any kind, you need to thank God. You need to thank Him that He has already given you everything you need to win the battle. Your goal isn't to add anything new to your spirit; your goal is to draw out what God has already put into your spirit.

> What can you thank God for today? (Remember to thank Him for everything!)

> _____

> _____

The book of Isaiah gives us the perfect directions for how to strap on our peace shoes. Isaiah 26:3 says, "You will keep in perfect peace those whose minds are steadfast, because they trust in you." When your mind agrees with God's mind—His truth and His standard—you will access God's power for victory in spiritual warfare. He will give you your peace shoes. Trusting God gives you peace.

Peace in the Presence of Problems

One of my favorite Bible stories shows the power of peace in the presence of problems—and potential pain! When Shadrach, Meshach, and Abednego were faced with the choice to bow down and worship their king as god or be thrown into a fiery furnace, the three boys stood by their principles and refused to bow. This was their response to

King Nebuchadnezzar's threat to throw them into the fiery furnace:

> King Nebuchadnezzar, we do not need to defend ourselves before you in this matter. If we are thrown into the blazing furnace, the God we serve is able to deliver us from it, and he will deliver us from Your Majesty's hand. But even if he does not, we want you to know, Your Majesty, that we will not serve your gods or worship the image of gold you have set up (Daniel 3:16-18).

God didn't keep these boys from the fire. They were thrown into it! In fact, God allowed Nebuchadnezzar to heat the furnace *seven times* hotter than it normally was. (Ouch!) And then God met Shadrach, Meshach, and Abednego in the fire. The Bible says that three men were thrown into the fiery furnace, but when the king went to look at them burning up, he saw four men walking around in the midst of the fire.

God didn't change their world. He joined them in it!

It's important for you to know that God won't always change your situation or your circumstances—although sometimes He does. When He does, that's one reason to praise Him. But even when He doesn't, if you are wearing the armor of God—which includes the shoes of peace— God will be right there beside you in the fiery furnace, and He will give you the peace you need to overcome your problems. Remember Isaiah 26:3—God promises to keep those in "perfect peace" whose minds are steadfast (which means *loyal* and *true*) because they trust in Him.

FLYING THROUGH THE STORM

A young boy was a passenger on an airplane flying through a terrible storm. The turbulence was causing the passengers to panic. However, the young boy was not afraid. One of the passengers next to the boy turned to him and asked, "How can you be so calm in the middle of all of this?"

The young boy replied, "My father is the pilot."

When you know who is at the controls, you have peace even in the middle of life's storms!

Every attack on peace in your life needs to be taken straight back to the spiritual realm and replaced with what God has to say on the matter. When you do that, you will wear shoes unlike those many others wear. You will wear shoes that let everyone—including Satan—know that you are covered by God's armor. You will walk without becoming weary, and in those shoes you will find the calming power of God's perfect peace.

LET'S TALK ABOUT IT

How does putting on the shoes of peace help you in spiritual warfare?

_____

_____

How is God's peace different from the world's peace? How does God give you His peace?

_____

_____

_____

How can putting on the shoes of peace help you to make good choices?

_____

_____

4

The **Shield**
of Faith

ow that we've taken a good look at the first three pieces of the armor of God, it's time to move on to the last three. The first three pieces are what you wear all the time. We are to *have* the belt of truth, *have* the breastplate of righteousness, and *have* the shoes of peace.

The next three pieces of armor—which we'll talk about in this chapter and the next two—are what you're supposed to have ready to pick up and use when you need them. The Bible tells us to "take up" the shield of faith, the helmet of salvation, and the sword of the Spirit.

If you are a baseball or softball player, you suit up in your team uniform before you play a ball game. You never remove your uniform during the game, but you do pick up your bat or your glove when you need them. Your team has the bats and gloves available to the players at all times, but it's your responsibility to grab them and use them when you need them. No one forces you to do that. And God doesn't force the shield of faith, helmet of salvation, or sword of the Spirit into our hands. Like the ball player's equipment, these three items are provided by God. They're always available, and in the Bible we find out how—and when—to use them.

Ephesians 6:16 says, "In addition to all this, take up the shield of faith, with which you can extinguish all the flaming arrows of the evil one." What exactly does a shield of faith look like? A Roman soldier's shield was pretty big—about two and a half feet wide and four feet long. (Sounds tough to carry, doesn't it?) It was big for a reason, though. The verb *shield* means *to protect* or *to cover*. In the heat of the battle, the soldier could crouch down and hide behind his shield when the enemy was shooting arrows at him.

In fact when a soldier was positioned correctly under the protection of his shield, he was so completely covered that he and other soldiers could link their shields together and hide behind whatever was thrown at them—arrows, javelins, or anything else!

So when does a Christian need to take up the shield of faith? We've heard this answer before: "Therefore put on the full armor of God, so that when the day of evil comes, you may be able to stand your ground" (Ephesians 6:13). But when exactly is this day of evil?

The day of evil is the worst day of your life—when everything you can imagine goes wrong. It starts out when you step in a mud puddle and get your brand-new shoes soaked and stained. It continues when your teacher hands out the test you forgot to study for. It gets worse when your best friend decides to ignore you all day long. And the very worst part happens when you get home and find out that your mom lost her job *and* your grandpa is in the hospital recovering from a heart attack.

It's on this day—what the Bible calls "the day of evil"—that you especially need to be covered by the shield of faith. You need protection you can count on because on this day you are most vulnerable to the arrows and javelins Satan is sending your way.

Have you ever had a day of evil? What happened on that day?

_____

_____

The Shield That Is Faith

The shield of faith can also be called the shield that *is* faith because the shield is actually faith itself. So in order to know what you're supposed to shield yourself behind, you need to figure out what faith is!

SOME WORDS ON FAITH

- Hebrews 12:2 tells us that Jesus is both the "pioneer and perfecter of faith."

- We read in Galatians 2:20, "I have been crucified with Christ and I no longer live, but Christ lives in me. The life I now live in the body, I live by faith in the Son of God, who loved me and gave himself for me."

- First John 5:4 says, "...for everyone born of God overcomes the world. This is the victory that has overcome the world, even our faith."

There are three key things you need to know about faith. The first thing is that Jesus is the perfect example of faith, from its creation to its perfection. The life of Jesus—everything He did, everything He said, and everything He was—is a perfect example of faith.

The second thing you need to know about faith is that if you have trusted in Christ and are saved by Him, you are positioned for victory because He lives in us. You're where you need to be!

Finally, the third thing you need to know about faith is that the key to overcoming anything you struggle with—your tendency to get mad and blow up, the way you worry, or your feelings of not being as good as others—is faith.

Faith sounds like a good thing to have, doesn't it?

But what is faith? The simplest answer I can give you is this: Faith is acting as if God is telling the truth (because He is!). It's acting as if something is so, even when it appears not to be so. And it's doing this because God said it and you believe it.

This brings us back to the first piece of the armor of God—the belt of truth. It's no surprise that the belt of truth is the first piece of armor listed because many of the other pieces are connected to truth in some way. If you don't know the truth—or if you don't act on the truth—the shield of faith will never work. In order to have faith, you have to know the truth and you have to respond to it. Even having a lot of faith doesn't help you if your faith isn't connected to the truth. Faith is only as valuable as the thing it's connected to.

Faith vs. Feelings

If faith is connected to your feelings, that faith will be empty faith. It won't help you at all. You might *feel* like you're totally full of faith, but you end up not doing anything in response to that faith because you don't really believe in what you say you feel. It's like saying you can ski down a mountain run, but then you just sit in the lodge drinking hot cocoa...or saying you can surf in the ocean, but then you just stay on the beach and make sand castles. Faith is all about taking action!

A person can actually feel very faith-filled but have absolutely no faith. And a person can actually feel faith-less but have a ton of faith! The person with a ton of faith may be willing to take a step of faith—or do an action in faith—simply because he or she believes that what God says is true. Faith is never based on how much faith you *feel*. It's always based on what you *do* in response to what you *believe*.

Faith is acting on the truth whether you feel the truth or not. It's acting on the truth whether you like the truth or not. It's also acting on the truth whether you agree with the truth or not. Faith shows up on your feet!

What is one thing you can do this week to act in faith?

_____

_____

TRUTH OVER FEELINGS!

Have you ever seen a movie that freaked you out just a little bit—or maybe more than a little bit? Now, you know those monsters or villains running around on the screen aren't real. You know that the action that makes your heart speed up isn't real. You know that the main character's scary situation isn't real. But even though you know all that, you sit through the movie and squirm, cover your eyes, and maybe even scream.

When you finally get into bed and try to go to sleep, you end up tossing and turning. Your mind is racing with scary scenes from the movie you just saw. You know it's not real. Yet your heart is still pounding, and every little noise makes you jump. Your feelings are responding as if you thought the movie might be real. This is because the filmmakers made you feel as if it were real. They manipulated the lighting, sound, and special effects to make everyone watching the movie feel like it was real.

You'll never get control of the movie's effect on your emotions until your mind gets control of your emotions. As long as you continue to feel like the movie was real, that movie can keep you awake all night—even though you know it isn't true. You need to put the truth before your feelings so you can get a good night's sleep and stop worrying!

Take the Next Step

So, at this point you know that it's important to have faith and that your faith needs to be based on what is true—not on what you feel. The next thing to do is to take a step, make a move, and do the thing that God has asked you to do without paying attention to the feelings that go along with it. So, you take the step and try to leave your feelings behind. But then guess what happens next. Your feelings follow you!

This might be a little hard to understand, so let me give you an example. The Bible says that you are to love your enemies and pray for those who treat you badly. If you choose by faith to do a kind action to someone you think of as your enemy—say, a kid who has been mean to you—your feeling of kindness toward that person will one day be stronger than the feelings of hatred, anger, or bitterness that you feel. Your feelings will eventually catch up with your actions if you continue to be kind to that person.

Now, this doesn't mean that being bullied is okay. Bullying takes many forms—physical as well as emotional— and all forms of bullying are hurtful. If someone is hurting you, you need to go right away and talk to an adult who can help you. But along the way, continue to show kindness to the person who's calling you names or trying to turn your friends against you. Do it through faith!

AN EXAMPLE OF FAITH

One of my favorite biblical illustrations of acting out in faith is found in the book of Luke. Jesus, from a boat, was teaching a group that had gathered near a lake to listen to Him. When He finished teaching, He told Peter—who was a fisherman—to take the boat out into deep water and let down the nets for a catch. Peter questioned Jesus by saying that they'd worked hard all night and hadn't caught anything.

"Oh, by the way," Peter continued, "we're also in shallow water right now—which, if You knew anything about fishing, You would realize is not the place to catch fish."

"Just cast the net on the other side," Jesus responded. "Do what I say, Peter."

Peter didn't think that Jesus' command made any sense. But, maybe even with a sigh or a huff, Peter did what Jesus said.

Guess what happened next? Peter and the other fishermen got the biggest catch of their lives! "When they had done so, they caught such a large number of fish that their nets began to break. So they signaled their partners in the other boat to come and help them, and they came and filled both boats so full that they began to sink" (Luke 5:6-7).

What an example of faith! On that amazing day, Peter and the other fishermen discovered what it meant to have faith. They acted on what Jesus said, in spite of what they already knew about fishing. And just look at the result!

All the Faith You'll Ever Need

Here's an important thing to remember: Faith doesn't make God move. What faith *does* do is access what God has already done. If you think that your faith is going to make

God move, all you're going to care about is getting more and more faith! However, as a Christian you already have all of the faith you're ever going to need to access anything God is going to do for you. Jesus said that faith the size of a mustard seed could move a tree or a mountain (Matthew 17:20; Luke 17:6). In other words and as the saying goes, "A little dab'll do ya."

So if you don't need more faith, what do you need? You need more truth!

Some people think that they need to do good works to access what God has in store for them in His grace. But our works actually just show our faith. Our works—the good things that we do—prove that we have faith.

Faith accesses grace. Works don't access grace, because once you attach works to grace, it's no longer grace. What is grace? Grace is a free gift from God, given to those who believe in Him. Grace is God's love and mercy given to you not because of anything you've done (good works) to earn it. It's given because God wants you to have it.

So we know that faith is all about truth, not all about feelings. We know that we don't have to do anything to get God's grace (His love and mercy). That brings us to the next question: How are we supposed to *use* the shield of faith? Habakkuk 2:4 says, "...the righteous person will live by his faithfulness." What does it mean to live by faith?

If you live by faith, it means that faith becomes your regular way of thinking, doing, and being. Faith isn't just saying, "Hey, I know that the shield of faith is there and it's mine to take whenever I want it. I'm just going to use it when I feel like it. It's kind of heavy to carry around otherwise."

If you have faith, you need to grab that shield and use

it to the max! This means that your faith shows up in the way you walk, talk, and live your life. It means that faith becomes your groove—your zone. The Bible is pretty direct in 2 Corinthians 5:7: "...live by faith."

How's Your Faith Walk?

Have you ever noticed that certain people have an easy-to-recognize way of walking or running? Maybe you see someone coming down the street, and you just *know* that it's your best friend because of the way she walks—almost like she's walking on her toes. Or you're looking for your brother in his cross-country race, and you can tell it's him because of the long strides he always takes. You recognize his stride before you even see his face!

The same thing should be true about Christians. We should have a "faith walk" (or a "faith run") that makes us look different from everyone else. It ought to be so distinct that others will recognize it before we even get close enough for them to see who we are.

The only way you can have a unique, one-of-a-kind faith walk that tells the world, "I belong to God!" is to remember that *faith is not a feeling*. Faith is an *action*. And faith is only as valuable as the object in which it is placed. You can have all the faith in the world that you can fly, but unless God makes you fly, you'll never get off the ground. Faith has to be connected to the truth, and the truth is connected to God.

My wife, Lois, won't fly on small airplanes. Her faith is small because the plane is small. Lois's faith grows when the size of the plane grows. Your view of God—how big you think He is—will decide the size of your faith.

The Bible tells us, "Now faith is confidence in what we hope for and assurance about what we do not see" (Hebrews 11:1). This verse means that if you can see something, you're not using faith. It's easy to believe in something you can see. God wants you to have faith even when you *can't* see something. He wants you to have faith that He's going to take care of you and will always be there for you.

How can you put your faith into action?

_____

_____

FAiTH SHOWS UP iN YOUR FEET

I enjoy watching the Olympics because they bring out the best in athletes. In the Olympics athletes push harder, go farther, and aim higher than they ever have before.

One scene in particular from the 1996 Olympics (well before you were born!) is forever etched in my mind. It's a scene you've probably seen in replays of amazing moments from past Olympic competitions. It happened on the final night of the women's gymnastics team event. The United States was in second place behind the Russians and needed a good score on the vault in order to beat them.

Kerri Strug stood on the mat as the final gymnast to vault for the Americans. The gymnast who had gone before Kerri had fallen on both of her vaults, so the Americans had to throw out her score. This meant that Kerri's score would have to count. Whether the Americans went home with gold, silver, or bronze was now up to Kerri. The weight of a nation rested on her 88-pound frame.

Kerri didn't have a reputation for being all that tough in the clutch. In fact she was known for buckling under pressure. Of the seven-member gymnastics team, she'd even earned the nickname "Baby," but the vault was her best event.

Kerri needed to score higher than a 9.4 on her final vault in order to give the Americans the gold, and she had two chances to do it. She fell on her first vault, spraining her ankle and tearing ligaments as well. A hush came over the crowd. How could Kerri vault again? She could barely walk!

Kerri's teammates urged her to try again as she limped back to the starting point. She fought back the tears filling her eyes. She knew that all of her teammates' hopes and dreams were in her last vault, but as she would say later on, she didn't even know if she could run, let alone vault. She considered walking away.

Yet the voice of her coach, Bela Karolyi, sealed her decision to stay. He yelled, "You can do it, Kerri! You can do it!" She looked at him, and she believed. And her feet demonstrated that belief.

After saluting the judges, Kerri ran toward

the vault—propelling herself one last time into the air. Hardly able to hold her foot down on the mat, she stuck her landing. Then she immediately collapsed on the mat in tears and agony. As she was carried down the stairs, Kerri's score went up. It was more than enough. The Americans had won. Kerri had grabbed the gold!

Later on Kerri revealed what pushed her to try one last time. She said, "When Bela looks at you and says you can do it, you know you can."

Faith. Kerri got the gold because faith showed up in her feet.

If a weight lifter can lift 500 pounds, will he have a problem carrying 25 pounds of groceries? Not at all! If he can handle the 500 pounds, he can handle the groceries. If Jesus Christ was able to overcome all the sin of the entire world on the cross—which He did—He can definitely take care of any situation you're in right now. Your assignment is to believe that Jesus can help you overcome your problems and then act on that belief. God has already given you enough power to do battle. He's already given you enough strength to fight. You just need the shield of faith!

God has given you the shield of faith to protect you from Satan. When you use it properly—as He taught you to use it in the Bible—you can advance against the enemy. That's because you'll be confident that God's Word and His promises are true.

When you're having your worst day ever, you might

wonder if things will ever be good again. Will you ever do well in school? Will your friends ever act like real friends? Will your family ever stop having problems?

Then God reminds you that He has never asked you to do anything that He is not totally and completely certain you can do through Him. If you listen closely, you might be able to hear His voice. He's saying, "You can do it! You can do it!"

Trust Him!

Pick up your shield of faith and with it grab the victory that has already been given to you!

LET'S TALK ABOUT IT

When do you need to take up the shield of faith?

_____

_____

What are three key things you need to know about faith?

_____

_____

What does it mean to live by faith? How can you start living by faith today?

_____

_____

5

The **Helmet** of Salvation

Y ou're almost fully dressed in the armor of God! You've put on the belt of truth, the breastplate of righteousness, the shoes of peace, and the shield of faith. You have just two pieces of armor to go—the helmet of salvation and the sword of the Spirit.

Remember, the helmet of salvation is one of the things you need to have ready to pick up—or as the Bible says, "take up"—whenever you need it.

What does a helmet do for you? The main purpose of a helmet—whether it's a soldier's helmet, a construction worker's hard hat, or a cyclist's aerodynamic helmet—is to protect the brain from injury.

For instance, a football player's helmet is padded on the inside to absorb the force when he gets pounded to the ground. The brain must be fiercely protected because once the brain becomes damaged, the body becomes damaged too.

Just as your brain is the control center for your body, your mind is the control center for your will and your emotions. Your mind needs to be protected with a helmet that's able to absorb the force of being hit by the enemy and even knocked to the ground. This happens all the time in spiritual warfare!

Listen for God's Voice

You need to wear the helmet of salvation so that you can keep your mind alert and tuned in to the sound of God's voice. Other people's voices—their opinions, thoughts, and suggestions—will often drown out what God is trying to say to you. It's not that other people are being unkind. They might even be trying to help you! It's just that, in the midst of battle, you need to be able to hear the voice of the One who is in charge. If you can't hear God clearly, the result will be defeat.

God is trying to speak truth into your mind, but Satan is trying to interrupt what God is saying. That's one big reason why God wants you to wear the helmet of salvation!

Your mind is really important. What you put into it—words, images, thoughts—has a direct impact on what you do and who you become. Proverbs 23:7 strongly warns us to guard our minds: "As he thinks within himself, so he is" (NASB). This means, quite simply, that we *do* what we *think*.

Have you ever played any of the newest virtual reality games? They're nothing short of amazing in how they show reality. In those games you can be sitting as still as a rock in the comfort of your own living room and think you're on a roller coaster because that's what you're seeing through your headset. Your stomach starts to feel like it's going to come up through your mouth exactly as if you were on a *real* roller coaster. You're not actually on the ride, of course, but the game makes you think you're on it. And because of that, you start moving, shifting, screaming, and responding just as if you were really on the ride.

Satan's game is to keep you from wearing the helmet of salvation. He wants what he shows you through his own headset to become the reality through which you interpret and respond to life. He wants to be the one in control of your game. You need to keep that helmet of salvation on your head so you can tune him out!

When a soldier goes into battle, he can't wear just any old thing on his head, like a baseball cap or a knit ski hat. He's supposed to wear a *helmet*. It's the same thing with the armor of God. You're not supposed to put any old thing on your head—or even any old helmet. It's specifically the *helmet of salvation* that you're supposed to wear. So what exactly is the *salvation* part of the helmet of salvation?

Salvation: Past, Present, and Future

Many people think that salvation simply means being born again. When you're born again, you have placed your trust in Christ for the forgiveness of your sins. When you do this, an all-of-a-sudden change occurs. This change is called *justification*. Justification is when God removes the penalty of (or punishment for) your sin—which is death—and gives you the gift of righteousness. So a big part of salvation *is* being born again and having new life through Christ. But salvation includes *all* that Christ has provided for you: past, present, and future.

So, *justification* is what happened the moment you were saved. That's the past tense of salvation. But did you know that your salvation is still happening in the present? The term for salvation that's happening in the present is *sanctification*. When God sanctifies you, He removes the power of sin over you as the Holy Spirit works in your life. And that brings us to the future part of salvation—*glorification*. That's when the presence of sin will completely be removed from your life.

Those are some pretty long words with some very deep thoughts! What you need to know at this point is that sanctification—the present form of salvation—is what we're going to focus on when we talk about the helmet of salvation. It's the *right now* time in your life, the time when you're becoming more and more like Christ.

Romans 1:16 says, "For I am not ashamed of the gospel, for it is the power of God for salvation to everyone who believes..." The word *salvation* in this verse means "to be delivered." Did you know that God's salvation can deliver you from hell in the present (during this life) as well as hell in the future (after you die)?

There are a number of things that God may need to deliver you from in your daily life—a bad friendship, a tendency to get mad, or laziness. These things can take control of your life and actually make your life hell on earth! And when they take control, Satan knows that all he has to do is push this or that button to get you to do or think something that you shouldn't.

But don't freak out! God has the power to deliver you and get you back walking with Him.

What are some of the bad things that can take control of your life?

_____

_____

> For it is by grace you have been saved, through faith—and this is not from yourselves, it is the gift of God—not by works, so that no one can boast. For we are God's handiwork, created in Christ Jesus to do good works, which God prepared in advance for us to do (Ephesians 2:8-10).

The Bible tells us that salvation is *by* grace, *through* faith, and *for* good works. All of these things are a part of salvation. You're supposed to walk the way you've been saved: "So then, just as you have received Christ Jesus as Lord, continue to live your lives in him" (Colossians 2:6). Unless you really understand what God means here, you'll be grabbing any old hat and shoving it on your head, hoping it works as a helmet against the enemy. I don't know about you, but when I'm in battle, I want more than a ball cap covering my head! I want something strong and hard. I want a helmet!

More About Grace

Let's talk more about grace. When we talk about grace, I want you to remember one thing: *Grace has nothing at all to do with you.* Instead, grace is all about what God has done *for* you. Grace includes everything that God has already provided for you.

Did you know that there's nothing God can do for you that He hasn't already done? It's true! There's nothing God can give you that He hasn't already given you.

GOD HAS DONE IT ALL!

Everything God is ever going to do for you has already been done!

- Every healing He will ever give you in your physical body has already been given.
- Every terrific opportunity He is ever going to open up for you has already been opened up.
- Every problem God is ever going to solve for you has already been solved.
- Every tough situation He's ever going to get you through, He's already gotten you through.

The joy you're seeking already exists. The peace you're wishing for is already present. The power you need to live the life God has created you to live, you already have. How can this be? Because God has already deposited in the heavenly realm "every spiritual blessing" you will ever need. It's all there waiting for you!

Have you ever struggled to feel thankful for the things you have? Your dad cooks terrific homemade pizza for dinner, but you'd rather eat at the gourmet pizza restaurant your best friend goes to every Friday night. You have plenty of jeans to wear—they fit you and they look nice—but the cool girls at school are wearing designer jeans that cost a hundred dollars or more, and you *really* wish you had just one pair. You're doing well on swim team—you keep decreasing your time in races and you're getting some ribbons at meets—but that one kid on your team who hardly shows up to practice wins almost every single race! Sometimes it's tough to feel thankful for the things you have—especially when someone else seems to have more than you.

What are some things that you struggle to feel thankful for?

_____

_____

You know that God has given you joy, but right now you're not feeling very joyful. You know that He's given you peace, but you just *can't* feel peaceful right now. How can you access—or get to—these things that God has already given you?

You're looking for God's grace, but you're not lacking grace or the things that grace supplies. The problem has to do with the way you access grace—through faith. You don't access grace by doing good things or by being a good person. The only access point to the grace that salvation supplies is faith.

It's like wearing a cloth baseball cap in place of the helmet of salvation. The cap might have your name on it, it might be your favorite color, and it might be the style that looks perfect on you, but it's the wrong hat! It's not the helmet of salvation, and so it provides you with no protection. Wearing the baseball cap is like trying to access grace through works. Grace has nothing to do with you or what you do. It is what God does for you because of His *unmerited favor*. This means that God has given you a gift that you don't deserve, but He has given it to you because He loves you.

Some people think that if they go to church more often, God will bless them more. Or if they give more money, they will get more money. Or if they treat their neighbors nicer, God will be nicer to them. But it doesn't work that way.

Going to church, giving money, and being nice are all

good things. Doing good things isn't the problem. The problem is with *why* you're doing good things. If you're doing them so God will like you more and give you more grace, that's not going to work.

When I was in school, I was determined to get A's in all my classes. In one particular class, I remember spending a ton of time on a certain paper. I was so confident that I was going to get an A on this paper! When I got it back, though, I was shocked to see a big zero written on the top of it. Scribbled underneath the zero were these words: "Great work. Wrong assignment."

A lot of people are working on the wrong assignment! We're saved by grace, through faith, and for good works that God prepared ahead of time. Our good works must flow out of God's work of grace in our lives rather than out of a heart that's trying to earn His favor or reduce His anger. God knows our hearts.

EARNING GOD'S LOVE

In a healthy home that functions the way God designed it, a child doesn't need to do anything to earn her parents' love. The parents already love that child unconditionally—no matter what the child says or does. There is nothing at all that the child can do to make her parents love her. She is already loved simply because she is their child.

We're like the child, and God is like the parents. No matter what we say or do, He loves us simply because He is our Father!

More Than Enough

I've been a pastor and a counselor for many years, and I know a lot of people don't realize this incredibly important thing: *God loves you*. God cannot love you any more than He already does. He showed that by sending His own son, Jesus Christ, to die for you. In that action He gave you all the love He could ever give you. Even if you try to make God love you more, you can't do it. His love is more than enough!

There is something that you *can* do with God's love, though. You can access His love through faith. Faith is your positive response to what God has already done. The good works you do express your faith; they don't earn you God's grace. So when you go to church and put money in the offering plate or show kindness to others, do these things not so you can earn God's favor, but as an expression of your faith in Him as your Savior.

TURN ON THE POWER!

Your home is connected to a local power company. This power company supplies your home with everything you need to run everything you have that requires electricity—your washer and dryer, your computer, and your lights. Let's say you turned off all the lights in your home and just sat there in the dark. It would be silly of you to call the power company and ask them to give you more power, wouldn't it? They've already given you all the power you need!

Instead, what you need to do is access that

power. You need to flip on the light switch, which opens up the flow of power.

In the spiritual realm, faith flips the switch and releases the flow of grace into our lives. In fact there's only one way to access grace—and that's through faith. So flip on the switch and turn on the power!

God gives us grace only in response to faith. Your good works merely reflect the fact that you believe what God says about grace. You do them in response to grace, not to try to get grace.

As soon as you realize that there's nothing you can do to get God to love you more, you'll discover the power for living a life of victory. You will have more confidence to do the right things, like standing up for a classmate who's being teased or putting more effort into your schoolwork or having a better attitude about doing your chores. In fact you will become a whole new you!

See Yourself as God Sees You

Do you ever look in the mirror and not like what you see? Maybe you think your hair is too curly or your nose is too big or your teeth are crooked. Do you want to know something amazing? God can change the way you look at yourself by showing you how He looks at you!

When you see yourself the way God sees you, you will begin to walk differently, talk differently, act differently, and live differently. You will live in the victory that God has already given to you.

How do you see yourself?

_____

_____

How does God see you?

_____

_____

A LiFE OF GRACE

The apostle Paul—who wrote much of the New Testament—spent years of his life sacrificing, working, and serving God, even when his own health and comfort suffered. (He even went to prison for God!) In 1 Corinthians 15:10, he said, "...by the grace of God I am what I am." In fact Paul's response to God's grace is what produced the good works in his life. Paul explains further, "...and his grace to me was not without effect. No, I worked harder than all of them—yet not I, but the grace of God that was with me."

Paul is saying that when he understood grace, he didn't get lazy. He didn't start sinning more. Not at all! When Paul understood all that God's grace had done for him, he wanted to work even harder because he was so thankful for it!

Grace should never make you lazy. It should, instead, make you more committed, obedient, generous, and enthusiastic because when you see all that God has done for you, you want to say thank you!

Know What Your Ticket Includes!

One day a man was given a special gift—a cruise! He had never been on a cruise before, so he was excited to take his first voyage. He didn't have to pay anything at all for the cruise. The person who gave it to him paid for the whole thing.

Throughout the week on the cruise, one of the crew members noticed that the man frequently ate the free crackers and juice provided on the deck. In fact he had never seen anyone eat as many crackers as this man did. Wondering why he was eating so many crackers and drinking so much juice, the crew member decided to ask the man.

"Sir, how did you enjoy the cruise?"

"It was spectacular!" the man replied. "I've never experienced anything like it before."

"Very good, sir," the crew member said. "I noticed that you really liked the crackers and juice on the deck. I was just wondering—why?"

"Well," the man replied, "I saw all of the lavish meals that were being offered all week long, but I didn't have any money. And since the crackers and juice were free, I decided to live on them during the cruise."

The crew member sighed. "Someone didn't give you all of the information! When your friend paid for your ticket, it not only included getting on the boat and going everywhere that the boat goes but also included everything on the boat as well. Your food was covered in the price of the ticket."

What disappointment this man must have felt! All that yummy food was right there for him—three meals a day plus snacks *and* dessert—yet all he ate were crackers and juice!

So be aware of what your ticket includes! Know what you get when you put on the armor of God. The helmet of salvation not only takes you to heaven but also supplies— by grace, through faith—everything you need while you're here on earth. When you understand the truth of salvation and wear it as a helmet, there's no limit to all of the awesome things God will do both in you and through you!

LET'S TALK ABOUT IT

What is the main purpose of a helmet? What does the helmet of salvation do for you?

_____

_____

What does salvation mean to you? How does God define salvation in the Bible?

_____

_____

What are some of the things that God has already done for you?

_____

_____

What are some positive things you can do to express your faith?

_____

_____

6

The **Sword** of the Spirit

This is it! The final piece of the armor of God! When you successfully put on, take up, and get going with all six pieces of the armor, you'll have all you need to experience true and lasting victory!

Ephesians 6:17 gives us the final piece: "Take...the sword of the Spirit, which is the word of God."

The sword of the Spirit stands out from every other piece of armor. The other five pieces are designed to protect you and hold you steady. The sword of the Spirit is the only offensive weapon in the armor. It's the only one designed for attacking the enemy.

Now, when you're imagining the sword of the Spirit, I want you to erase from your mind the image of Zorro or the swashbuckling pirates you've seen in the movies. That's not the kind of sword we're talking about here.

If you were to draw a picture of the sword of the Spirit, it would look more like a dagger—about a foot and a half long and used for up-close, in-your-face, hand-to-hand combat. You'd be in a duel with a single opponent—just you against the enemy. And what a weapon it is! If it were a real-life weapon, its blade would be double-edged and its point would be needle sharp. Easy to hide, it could be quickly pulled out and used to deliver a deathblow straight to the opponent's heart. Sounds pretty powerful, doesn't it?

When God tells you to take up the sword of the Spirit, He knows that you'll find yourself in situations where the enemy is right in your face, like a basketball player trying to block your shot.

Handle with Care!

It's really important to remember that this is the sword of the *Spirit*. It's not your own personal sword. It's not your youth pastor's sword. It isn't even the church's sword. It's the *Spirit's* sword. The Bible tells us that this is the only weapon that is used in the spiritual realm.

If it's the only one, it must be incredibly important!

And it's something to be handled with care. Because it's the Spirit who uses this sword in the heavenly places to deliver a deathblow to the enemy (Satan), you can't deliver the deathblow yourself. If you grab the sword on your own and try to do it yourself, you're going to fail. This is because the sword of the Spirit needs to be handled in a very specific way.

You can't use the sword of the Spirit in the usual human way. Moses learned this when he tried to deliver Israel in his own strength. Peter learned this when he cut off the ear of one of the soldiers who had come to arrest Jesus.

When you choose a manmade method in a spiritual battle, you cancel out God's power in your fight. The Bible even gives us a warning about this: "Do not take revenge, my dear friends, but leave room for God's wrath" (Romans 12:19).

You need to let go of your own approach to fighting, which includes letting go of the way you respond to things emotionally. What's your natural reaction when someone gets mad or yells at you? You probably start to feel upset inside and quite possibly get mad right back at them!

How do you respond when someone gets mad at you?

_____

_____

Instead of using your own approach—which doesn't work *at all* in the spiritual realm!—you need to use God's approach. Your job is to put on His full armor and listen to His command.

There is so much power in the sword of the Spirit! God gave it to you as the only piece of offensive—or attack—weaponry in the entire armor. Maybe this sword is the only offensive piece in the collection because it is the only offensive piece you need!

When you imagine a sword, you think of a metal weapon with a sharp blade and a super sharp point, don't you? Maybe you're imagining a Samurai sword or a long Middle-Ages weapon. And there's also that dagger that we were talking about earlier—what the sword of the Spirit might look like if it were an earthly weapon. Remember, though, that this is *spiritual* armor. It's not *physical* armor. Things look different in the spiritual world. So what kind of sword are we *really* talking about?

The Bible tells us that the sword of the Spirit is the Word of God. And the Word of God is the Bible. So the sword of the Spirit is the Bible—a book! How can a book—even a book as amazing as the Bible—be a weapon?

Three Different Words for the Same Thing

If you were to read the New Testament in the Greek language, you would discover three different words for the Word of God—*graphe*, *logos*, and *rhema*. You probably have no idea what those words mean, but that's okay. We're going to go through them together, and you're going to discover some amazing truths about God's Word.

You've probably worked with graphs in math class—bar graphs or line graphs or even pie graphs. You read the graph to find out information about something. And you know what an autograph is, don't you? It's your signature. The Greek word *graphe* means the *writings* of God (what God told other people to write down). It's the actual book of God—the Bible. When your Sunday school teacher tells you to turn to the book of John in your Bible, what you hold in your hands and turn the pages of is the *graphe*.

Whether you have the *graphe* on your nightstand, in your backpack, or on your bookshelf, what you have is an actual book that you can touch. It's the Word of God in written form. But when the Bible tells you to take the sword of the Spirit—which is the Word of God—it's not talking about the *graphe* meaning.

Yes, there's power in the Bible, but the power isn't in the paper and ink. Some people think there is, though. They think that carrying their Bible around with them will somehow protect them or make their life better. But that's just superstition—like carrying around a lucky penny. If you never open that Bible and never take into your heart what's inside, it won't do you any good!

The second Greek term for the Word of God is *logos*. You've probably seen logos all over. The Nike swoosh is a logo. Your favorite breakfast cereal has a logo on the package. Cars—Subarus, Toyotas, Fords—are marked with logos. When you see a familiar logo, you instantly know the brand of the clothing or food or vehicle. You get the whole message in one quick image.

In the Bible, *logos* refers to the *message* of the book. It's the meaning of the words. *Logos* is a very powerful word. John 1:1 says, "In the beginning was the Word, and the Word was with God, and the Word was God." Jesus is called the Logos in this verse because He was sent as God's messenger to tell the whole world about God. He was sent to carry God's message of love and salvation to us.

In Hebrews 4:12, God tells us more about the Logos (message): "For the word of God is alive and active. Sharper than any double-edged sword, it penetrates even to dividing soul and spirit, joints and marrow; it judges the thoughts and attitudes of the heart."

So the message—or the Logos—is more than just words on paper. The Logos is alive and active! It's a force with energy behind it. We're talking about serious energy here! God says that it is "sharper than any double-edged sword." Ouch! That kind of sword could go deeper and further than any kind of real-life sword. This sword—a spiritual sword—goes so deep that it can pierce between the soul and the spirit in the invisible—or spiritual—realm. Take my word for it—that's really deep!

When the sword divides between the soul and the spirit, God is able to work more freely in your life. The sword divides all the things in your soul—negative thoughts, bad habits, intense emotions—that get in the way of your understanding the truth of the Spirit.

The Logos is not only able to penetrate the invisible realm and divide between soul and spirit. It's also able to discern and judge both the thoughts and the intentions of your heart. It doesn't simply address the action, but deals with your heart and mind, which drives the action. It doesn't just say, "Forgive your friend," or "Turn off the TV and start doing your homework," or "Don't listen to that song." It goes deeper and focuses on the *why* behind the *what*.

Why should you forgive your friend? Because God forgave you, and He wants you to live in peace with others. Why should you turn off the TV and start doing your homework? Because God wants you to make good use of your time. He has a wonderful plan for your life, but you need to be obedient before He can reveal that plan. Why shouldn't you listen to that song? Because its negative message will soak into your mind and put thoughts in your head that aren't glorifying to God. There's always a *why* behind the *what*!

SEEING WHAT'S ON THE INSIDE

Have you ever broken a bone—or thought you've broken a bone—and gone to the doctor's office to get an X-ray? You can't tell from the outside if the bone is broken, but the X-ray takes a picture that shows what the bone looks like on the inside.

Hebrews 4:13 says, "Nothing in all creation is hidden from God's sight. Everything is uncovered and laid bare before the eyes of him to whom we must give account." The Word of God opens you up to reveal all the things inside you. It exposes you like a spiritual X-ray machine, showing the inner truth that outward actions don't always reveal.

A person can have great actions but also have a bad heart. They might simply be doing those great actions because they don't want to get punished or they're afraid of looking bad. And another person can have bad actions but have a right heart, making poor decisions but being fully aware of his or her need for Jesus' love and forgiveness.

So, don't judge by what you see on the outside. Only God can read the X-ray and see what's inside a person's heart!

Jesus looks past what can be seen on the outside and focuses on what's deep inside your heart. As you work to understand God's truth and allow the Logos—the message of God—to penetrate and take root deep within you, it will reveal your heart to such a degree that you're able to see right from wrong and understand truth from lie. God's Word will penetrate you deeply, making a huge difference in your life.

That brings us to the third term in the Bible for the Word of God—*rhema*. When God tells us to "take...the sword of the Spirit, which is the word of God," He's not talking about *graphe* or *logos*. He's talking about *rhema*.

So you need to know what *rhema* is!

Rhema means the *spoken* word, or what has been *declared*.

THREE MEANINGS OF THE WORD

- *Graphe* is the written word.
- *Logos* is the message of the written word.
- *Rhema* is the spoken word.

You could own a Bible factory and publish millions of Bibles every day but never have the power of the sword of the Spirit. You could study God's Word 24 hours a day and know the Scriptures backward and forward but still not be able to use the power of the sword against the enemy. You need the *rhema* of God—the one offensive weapon given to you.

A lot of Christians get stuck on *graphe*. They bring their Bibles to church every week or carry them around everywhere they go, but the Bible is just a book until you open it, read it, and listen to God teaching you through it.

Some Christians are stuck in Logos-land. They take notes on every sermon and never miss a Bible study, but they haven't used what they've learned against the enemy in spiritual warfare.

So what exactly is *rhema*?

Have you ever memorized a Bible verse or read a certain story in the Bible over and over until you felt like you totally knew it? And then one day, as you read or hear this familiar verse or that familiar story, you feel like God has marked it with a yellow highlighter pen especially for you. One verse, one word, or one truth leaps off the page and *totally* relates to a situation you're facing at home or in school. That's a *rhema*—God speaking directly to you out of His written Word.

God's spoken Word is so powerful that it's enough to create something out of nothing. Genesis 1:3 says, "And God said, 'Let there be light,' and there was light." Over and over in the beginning of Genesis, we read that God said that something was so, and it came to be so. All God had to do was speak the Word, and whatever He spoke happened! The *rhema* was the Spirit's dagger—or sword—that God used to create the world.

Can you imagine being able to create something just by speaking and commanding it to exist? That's how powerful God's spoken Word is! And we have access to it when we put on the full armor of God. That's why it's so important to study God's Word, learn it, and hide its truths deep in your heart. That's why it's so important to go to Sunday school or youth group and discover more about Jesus. That's why it's so important to ask your parents or your Sunday school teacher or your small group leader to explain the things you don't understand.

What can you do to discover more about *rhema*—God's spoken Word?

_____

_____

Getting the Word Straight

Because God's Word is so powerful, Satan knows that all he has to do is twist God's Word, and it will become a dull sword that you can't use. So, you need to understand the truth of what God is really saying to you in the Bible. You do this by reading and studying the Bible and memorizing verses, praying, and asking God and others to help you understand it.

When Adam and Eve sinned in the garden, Satan twisted God's Word by questioning Eve: "Did God really say...?" (see Genesis 3:1). He did this because he knew that if he could mix up the Word and confuse Eve, it would reduce God's power to defeat him.

Satan loves it when you say things like, "Well, I think..." or "Well, my opinion is..." He loves it every time you say, "My dad said..." or "My teacher said..." or "My friend said..." He loves to hear these words because he knows there's no power in what you think or feel or in what your family or friends say. He'll gladly leave you alone and let your mind be filled with ideas and opinions from hit movies and TV shows, popular songs and bestselling books, and text messages and Instagram posts. Satan loves it when you fill your mind with the things of the world. It makes his job easy!

What are some of the things of the world that you fill your mind with?

_____

_____

_____

What can you fill your mind with instead?

_____

_____

But as soon as you start saying, "Well, God says..." and begin to jab the sword of the Spirit directly into Satan's midsection, that's when he starts running. Satan can't stand straight against the powerful force of God's Word.

Jesus gives us a great example of the right way to use the sword of the Spirit. Matthew 4:1 says, "Then Jesus was led by the Spirit into the wilderness to be tempted by the devil." Do you want to hear something really crazy? It was God Himself who led Jesus straight into the face of the devil!

Why would God do something like that? Because He knew that Jesus was trained and ready to use the sword of the Spirit. He was confident that Jesus knew how to use the only offensive weapon in the entire armor of God to overcome the enemy.

Jesus had been fasting—not eating any food—for 40 days. When was the last time you ate something? (And you're probably hungry again, right?) Can you imagine not eating for 40 days? You wouldn't have any energy left! So, here was Jesus at his absolute weakest point, and guess what the devil tempts him with. That's right—food! In Luke 4:3, he tells Jesus, "If you are the Son of God, tell this stone to become bread."

Jesus, however, responded by saying, "It is written, 'Man shall not live on bread alone.'"

What Jesus _didn't_ do in this situation is just as important as what He _did_ do. By saying "it is written" and then using the full force of the Word of God, Jesus didn't get into a big argument or long discussion with Satan. He simply said "it is written" and followed up with what God had said. That's all He needed to do!

Satan wasn't done yet, of course. He came at Jesus two more times, tempting Him in a moment of physical weakness. Each time Jesus responded in the same way—"It is written"—followed by quoting what the Word said.

Jesus did have a real physical need here. He was hungry. Starving probably! Satan didn't twist Jesus' need—he didn't need to. Hunger is a pretty intense thing. Instead, what Satan did was try to twist the way Jesus went about meeting that need. He tempted Jesus to find fulfillment apart from God. However, when Satan did that, Jesus responded in a way that we might describe today as Googling God's feeding program. He told Satan—straight from the Word— what God says about bread and hunger. And that took care of that!

After only three times of Jesus responding with "it is written," Satan left. He couldn't handle more than three strikes, so he was out of there as quickly as he'd come.

Satan can hang out with you all day and all night if he knows you will never read the *graphe* (the actual Bible), which will help you understand the *logos* (the message of the Bible), which in turn will help you use the *rhema* (the spoken Word of God) that God has given to you to use whenever you need it. The sword of the Spirit is your offensive weapon— given to you by God—to advance against the enemy and win the battle. Romans 8:37 says, "in all these things we are more than conquerors through him who loved us."

When you can use the sword of the Spirit against the

enemy who is seeking to destroy you, it doesn't matter how old you are or how weak you seem. All you need to believe is that the sword in your hand is capable of doing more than you will ever need it to do. As we saw with Jesus in the wilderness, that sword will make the devil flee. I guarantee it. Better yet, God guarantees it. So grab the sword of the Spirit and use it on your path to living in ultimate spiritual victory!

LET'S TALK ABOUT IT

Why does the sword of the Spirit need to be handled in a very specific way? How are you supposed to handle it?

_____

_____

What are the three meanings of the Word of God? Which meaning refers to the sword of the Spirit?

_____

_____

How much power does God's spoken Word have? How can you understand what it means?

_____

_____

7
Victory!

A world champion body builder went to Africa on a tour to promote good health and physical fitness. He visited some large cities as well as some nearby villages where the people did not have access to electricity, television, or running water.

One day as the body builder was holding a fitness awareness seminar in a remote village, he had an interesting interruption. He had just finished demonstrating all the different ways he could cause his muscles to bulge and contract when the local tribal chief stopped him.

"What you have shown us is impressive," the tribal chief said. "I have never seen that many muscles on one man before."

The body builder, used to hearing such flattering remarks, smiled smugly. But the tribal chief continued talking. He said, "I have only one question. What do you use those muscles for?"

The body builder answered, "Body building is my profession. This is my job."

"You don't use those muscles for anything else?"

"No," replied the body builder.

"What a waste," said the chief, shaking his head slowly. "What a waste to have all of those muscles and not use them!"

Any Christian who has access to the full armor of God but doesn't use it is like the body builder. If you don't put on the armor, you'll never experience the victory. You'll never know what it's like to have access to God's power and to live completely for Him. But if you do use the armor of God on a daily basis, you *will* walk in victory!

Here's something really important to know about spiritual warfare: *Whatever is bothering you in the physical realm is coming from the spiritual realm.* The problems you're having right now are happening because spiritual warfare is happening. Satan doesn't want you to know that, though. He wants you to keep thinking that your impossible math teacher is the problem. He wants you to keep thinking that your on-again, off-again friend is the problem. He wants you to keep thinking that you yourself are the problem!

But those things *aren't* the problem. The problem is that there's a battle being fought in the spiritual realm—out there where you can't see it—and you're focusing on the things that you *can* see instead!

After you have on the full armor of God—the belt of truth, the breastplate of righteousness, the shoes of peace, the shield of faith, the helmet of salvation, and the sword of the Spirit—the next step involves prayer. Ephesians 6:18 says we are to "pray...on all occasions and with all kinds of prayers and requests. With this in mind, be alert and always keep on praying for all the Lord's people."

A lot of people don't really understand prayer. It's okay

if you're having a hard time figuring it out too. You're not alone!

For a lot of people—even for some Christians—prayer is kind of just a habit. They say a prayer before they eat a meal, but they don't really think about what they're saying. They say a prayer before bedtime, but they've said it so many times that they can say it without even thinking. Prayer should be much more than that. When you really understand prayer, it will affect how you live, what you pray, whether you pray, and what you expect will happen when you pray.

Prayer is going to God and asking for His divine intervention—His heavenly help—for what's going on in your world. You go to Him knowing that His Word is the truth and that He has all the power you need to experience victory.

Did you know that there are many things God *can* do but *doesn't* do simply because He has not been requested to do them? Your job is to go to God and ask for His help based on His Word, His truth, His promises, and His character (who He is). His job is to step in and help in response to your faith, your desire for Him, your submission to Him, and your acknowledgment of your need for Him. Imagine a little child trying to pour a glass of juice. Unless he asks his parent to help him, he's going to make a mess! But once he asks, the parent willingly pours the juice for him.

Of course, when you're facing a problem, you can choose to leave God out. He's given you that option. You can do things on your own—without God—all day long. But you can also invite Him into your life and watch Him show up in ways you've never imagined. You do that through prayer.

James 5:16 says, "Therefore confess your sins to each

other and pray for each other so that you may be healed. The prayer of a righteous person is powerful and effective." The Bible doesn't say that prayer *might* help. It clearly says that the prayer of a righteous person is *powerful* and *effective*. (Sounds pretty good, doesn't it?) That righteous person is you—who is saved by Christ, has a heart for God, and focuses on Him.

The Best Kind of Secret

Have you ever been told a secret? There are good kinds of secrets—the birthday gift you're giving your sister, the surprise trip to Disneyland your parents are planning, or the breakfast-in-bed you're making for your mom. There are also bad kinds of secrets—telling someone else what a friend confided to you (after you promised you wouldn't tell anyone), hiding the fact that you cheated on a test, or not telling your parents that you got in trouble at school. The Bible tells us that God has secrets that He's willing to share with you and me. I can guarantee you that these secrets are all good. In fact, they're the best kind of secrets—even better than the surprise trip to Disneyland!

God wants you to be so close to Him that He can lean over and whisper His secrets in your ear. We read in Psalm 25:14, "The LORD confides in those who fear him; he makes his covenant known to them."

When God reveals His secrets—His promises in His Word—to you, you will be able to take God's Word and send it right back to Him. That is when you can say, "God, You said in Your Word..." (Do you remember Jesus saying "it is written..." when Satan tempted Him in the wilderness?)

Now, it's important to remember that prayer isn't simply

seeing something you want and then claiming—or demanding—it. If God didn't tell you He's going to give you that awesome bright green mountain bike with all the bells and whistles, then you can pray until you're blue in the face and that bright green mountain bike will be sold to some other kid. *The main part of prayer is knowing what God already said.* A great place to start finding this out is in the Bible. God has given you literally *thousands* of promises in His Word!

Right now, you're spending a lot of your life learning—figuring out math problems, practicing writing skills, discovering new things about science, and maybe even learning to speak another language. Along with all of your school learning, it's important that you take the time to learn and know God's Word. If you don't understand what God is saying in the Bible, you'll never understand how you're supposed to talk to Him through prayer. You'll end up repeating empty prayers that don't have any meaning at all. Or you'll start asking for—and maybe even demanding—things that God never intended to give you. Either way you'll end up shoving the armor of God into the back of your closet or under your bed and saying, "It didn't work for me." Then you'll call or text someone or meet up with a friend or try to figure it out on your own—without God. And that's never going to work.

So you know that it's really important that you pray, but *when* should you pray? Ephesians 6:18 says that we should "pray in the Spirit on all occasions," but how is that possible? How are you supposed to pray *all* the time? How can you pray while you're taking a math test? How can you pray when you're talking to a friend? And is it even possible to pray while you're sleeping?

What God's Word is saying is that you're supposed to pray at specific, opportune times—like when the enemy is right in your face and everything is falling apart. Now, you aren't *just* supposed to pray when things are at their worst. You should be praying and thanking God in *all* circumstances—when things are going really well and life is just humming along normally. But when you find yourself really sad or hurting or scared, that's the time to suit up in the armor of God and pray!

What can you pray for when things are going well?

_____

_____

What can you pray for when things are falling apart?

_____

_____

How Do I Do This Prayer Thing?

Now for a lot of people, prayer seems kind of boring. But that's only because they don't understand what's happening in the invisible realm as a result of their prayers! If we could truly grasp all that happens in the invisible realm in response to our prayers, talking to God would be the top priority in all of our lives. We would do what the Bible urges us to do—pray all the time.

If you don't realize that your battles are being fought in the spiritual realm—where you can't see them—you might be tempted to think that God hasn't heard you or that He doesn't care about your problems. But God *does* hear your prayers—as soon as you offer them! And He *does* respond immediately to them. So why don't you get an answer right away?

Can you think of a battle or war that's lasted for only one minute? You can't! Some wars go on and on—even for a hundred years! Yet sometimes we say our prayer, wait about a minute for God's response, and then give up and do our own thing because God hasn't immediately responded.

God *does* hear your prayers. And if what you're praying is in line with what God says in His Word—the truth—you don't need to keep asking Him over and over and over again. After you ask Him, the rest of your prayer should be focused on thanking God for His promised response. And since demons—Satan's soldiers—are trying to block the delivery of that answer in your life, you should also ask God to step into the situation and prevent Satan from delaying your answer.

You're also supposed to pray on the alert—with your eyes wide open. You don't have to *physically* open your eyes. Sometimes it's easier to concentrate when your eyes are closed. But you *do* need to be looking for anything that Satan will use to stop you from praying.

Have you ever noticed that sometimes when you pray, a bunch of distractions show up? Your phone rings. Your brother barges into your room. Your own mind wanders. Or maybe you get sleepy even though you weren't sleepy before you started praying. Satan will try every trick in the book to stop you from praying. Why? Because prayer is the strongest tool in the armor of God.

What are some things that distract you from talking to God?

_____

_____

If the enemy is trying to distract you from praying, that's a good sign! But don't let Satan intimidate you or keep you from praying fervently in the Spirit. When you've suited up in the armor of God for battle, prayer is the ticket that takes you straight into the heart of it.

Did you know that God has already answered many of the things you've asked Him for in prayer? The problem is that Satan is now attempting to block God's answer from reaching you. But don't give up! And don't spend your time focusing on what has already been done. Instead thank God for what He has promised and keep praying until the moment arrives when you will receive your victory!

Under God's Umbrella

Not long ago I was walking in New York City when it began to rain. I had seen the weather report, so I had my umbrella ready. Several other people must have seen the report as well because they had their umbrellas too. But many people didn't have umbrellas. Those people rushed around looking for cover. Needless to say, they became cold and miserable as the rain drenched them!

Being underneath an umbrella doesn't stop the rain—it simply stops the rain from soaking you. The umbrella doesn't still the storm. What the umbrella *does* do is change the way in which the storm affects you.

Standing firm as you wear the armor of God doesn't stop the spiritual warfare from raging. It *does* stop it from defeating you. That's why one of the devil's schemes is to get you to step out from underneath the protective armor God has given you. Once you step out from underneath God's protection, you expose yourself to everything Satan brings your way. And the devil wants to drench you!

One of Satan's tactics is to get you to believe that God's covering isn't enough for the tsunami-sized disaster he's going to throw at you. He tries to get you to run. He wants you to drop your umbrella—your armor—and run someplace where you think you might be safer. But the key to victory in spiritual warfare comes when you recognize the truth that Jesus Christ has already secured the victory you seek. Your job, then, is to stand firm in that victory. *There is no safer place you or I could ever be than fully armed in our identity with Christ.*

KNOWING HOW IT ENDS

If you were to come to my house during football season, you would see that the NFL Network is always on my TV. Anyone who knows me at all knows that I love football! The great thing about the NFL Network is that it shows you the scores of every game of all 32 teams in the NFL each week. This is so you can know how everything ended. But there's something else that the NFL Network does. It also replays the games. So if you didn't happen to see the score, you wouldn't know how the game ended. But if you did see the score, even though you would already know how the game ended, you wouldn't know how it got to that point.

When I'm watching a football game and I already know how it ends, that changes the entire experience. I might see my team fumble, but I don't get upset because I know where the game is going. I might see my quarterback throw an interception, but I don't get nervous because I know how the game will end. At halftime, my team might be losing, but it doesn't matter. Sure, I may get a little frustrated, but I don't lose my temper. I don't stress. Why not? Because I've already seen the final score!

Jesus Christ has already secured your victory over anything that Satan throws at you. When you realize that, it takes the pressure off and frees you to play the game confidently in the strength of the One who has already won.

I can imagine what you might be saying right now: "This is a lot to remember, especially when I'm having my worst day ever! I can't even remember all six pieces of armor, let alone how to use them. Give me something simple!"

If you're in a crunch—if the "day of evil" is upon you and Satan and his demons are all up in your face—and you need help immediately, just remember this one thing: *Remember*

Jesus Christ. Right now I'm going to give you some verses that will take you through each piece of armor and help you to focus on Jesus:

The Belt of Truth

"I am the way and the truth and the life" (John 14:6).

Remember Jesus.

The Breastplate of Righteousness

"God made him who had no sin to be sin for us, so that in him we might become the righteousness of God" (2 Corinthians 5:21).

Remember Jesus.

The Shoes of Peace

"Therefore, since we have been justified through faith, we have peace with God through our Lord Jesus Christ" (Romans 5:1).

Remember Jesus.

The Shield of Faith

"...fixing our eyes on Jesus, the pioneer and perfecter of faith. For the joy set before him he endured the cross, scorning its shame, and sat down at the right hand of the throne of God" (Hebrews 12:2).

Remember Jesus.

The Helmet of Salvation

"Salvation is found in no one else, for there is no other name under heaven given to mankind by which we must be saved" (Acts 4:12).

Remember Jesus.

The Sword of the Spirit, Which Is the Word of God

"In the beginning was the Word, and the Word was with God, and the Word was God. He was with God in the beginning....The Word became flesh and made his dwelling among us. We have seen his glory, the glory of the one and only Son, who came from the Father, full of grace and truth....No one has ever seen God, but the one and only Son, who is himself God and is in closest relationship with the Father, has made him known" (John 1:1-2,14,18).

Remember Jesus.

In other words, if you can't remember anything else about the armor, *remember Jesus.*

In Jesus you have the belt of truth, the breastplate of righteousness, the shoes of peace, the shield of faith, the helmet of salvation, and the sword of the Spirit, which is the Word of God. When you know that Jesus is your advocate and your defender, all you need to say to the enemy is this: "Step aside, Satan, because it is time for Jesus Christ. He has me covered. He has my back!"

Even if you're feeling overwhelmed, you're totally stressed out, and you can't remember every piece of armor, *remember Jesus.* Without Him, the armor won't do you any good anyhow. But with Him, you are victorious!

Now, if you feel like Satan is running your life, feelings, and emotions, and if he's influencing your decisions, that means you've taken off your armor. It's time to put it on again. With the armor of God firmly in place, you'll be able to handle whatever Satan throws at you.

Please know that God does not dress you in the armor. It's your job to dress yourself! In grace He has given you everything you need to put on in faith. Faith is reaching into grace and grabbing what God has graciously given you through Christ. For example let's say it was a sunny day at the beach. If I bought you a pair of sunglasses to wear, but you didn't bother putting them on, they wouldn't do you any good. You would just keep squinting into the sun.

The armor of God has been completely supplied for you. Your victory has been completely provided, but until you grab it in faith, it does you no good. However, when you *do* grab it in faith, you'll quickly know that it was given by God because your life will change in such a way that only God could change it. Problems that you've been struggling with for a long time can be changed overnight when things are done God's way!

You know that God has stepped in when something you've been struggling with for a long time suddenly changes. You know it's the power of God at work when one day out of the blue, you aren't interested in listening to that music or watching that TV show anymore. You know it's the power of God when you find yourself drawn to better friends—friends who love God and will help you grow in your walk with Him. You know it's the power of God when you stop worrying about things that will probably never, ever happen.

When you suit up in the armor of God, you have the power to defeat the enemy. You can live in the victory Christ secured for you because when you trusted in Him, He crossed you over into a whole new realm. You have a new name—son or daughter of the living God. You have a new love—the Trinity of God the Father, God the Son, and God the Holy Spirit. You have a purpose and a destiny—to glorify God in all that you do while making a difference in the world. And you have new clothes—a belt, a breastplate, shoes, a shield, a helmet, and a sword. Wear them and win!

Satan is coming at you in this new realm, but when you operate according to the authority that God has given to you in the heavenly realm, you overcome the enemy because "the one who is in you is greater than the one who is in the world" (1 John 4:4). Your side—God's side—has won!

LET'S TALK ABOUT IT

What does prayer mean to you? What have you learned in this book that can help you when you pray?

_____

_____

_____

Sometimes God doesn't answer our prayers right away. What can we do while we wait for an answer?

_____

_____

_____

What do you need God's help with today? How can putting on the armor of God help you?

_____

_____

_____

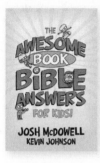

The Awesome Book of Bible Answers for Kids

Josh McDowell & Kevin Johnson

Kids are curious about Jesus and God and yet, by the time they are teens, the majority stop asking questions about faith and start questioning faith altogether. Respected Christian apologist Josh McDowell encourages children to stand on the foundation of truth with this contemporary gathering of concise, welcoming answers for kids ages 8 to 12.

A fun format includes key Bible verses and pre-teen friendly explorations of topics that matter most to kids:

- God's love and forgiveness
- Right and wrong and making choices
- Jesus, the Holy Spirit, and God's Word
- Different beliefs and religions
- Church, prayer, and sharing faith

The next time a child asks "Who is God?" parents, grandparents, and church leaders will want this practical and engaging volume handy. Helpful tips and conversation ideas for adults will help them connect with kids hungering for straight talk about faith in Jesus.

Bible Basics for Kids
An Awesome Adventure Through God's Word
Terry Glaspey & Kathleen Kerr

Do your kids have questions about God, the Bible, and faith? Perfect. Those questions are just the ticket to rock-solid answers in this fun and easy-to-understand book about the Bible. Kids ages 7-11 will find speedy summaries of *every* book of Scripture and a 90-day reading plan so they can explore Bible stories for themselves anytime.

Plus there are fabulous bonus features:

- a five-minute overview of the entire Bible— no kidding!
- tips and tricks for memorizing Bible verses
- silly riddles, Bible knock-knock jokes, and more

Spoiler alert: Your kids will have a blast, all the while discovering how all the Bible stories come together into one *big* story about God reaching out to His children through Jesus. And He can't wait for them to reach back...especially with questions!

One-Minute Mysteries and Brain Teasers
Good Clean Puzzles for Kids of All Ages
Sandy Silverthorne & John Warner

Readers of all ages will enjoy the challenge of discovering the answers to—or being stumped by—these interactive mysteries. In brief paragraphs and black-and-white illustrations, award-winning author Sandy Silverthorne and John Warner present 70 puzzles, each with a logical "aha" answer that requires thinking outside the box. Clues and answers are included in separate sections.

Mystery:

A man is looking at a clock that displays the correct time, but he doesn't know what time it is. Why not?

Clues:

- The man can see and tell time perfectly well.
- The clock is normal and in plain sight.
- More than one clock is in the room.

Solution:

Each clock in the room is displaying a different time, so he doesn't know which one is correct.

Hours of wholesome entertainment is practically guaranteed!

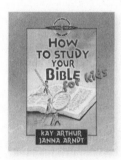

How to Study Your Bible for Kids
Kay Arthur & Janna Arndt

Based on Kay Arthur's bestselling *How to Study Your Bible* (390,000 copies sold), this easy-to-use Bible study combines a serious commitment to God's Word with fun illustrations, games, puzzles, and activities that reinforce biblical truth. *How to Study Your Bible for Kids* introduces the basics of inductive Bible study—observation, interpretation, and application—to children ages 9 to 12. As they learn about the people in the Bible, the way things were done in biblical times, the amazing miracles performed, and numerous terrific adventures found in the Bible, young people will discover that God's Word speaks to them right where they're at. They'll come away from this study with a deeper understanding of God's love and care for them.

To learn more about Harvest House books and
to read sample chapters, visit our website:

www.harvesthousepublishers.com

HARVEST HOUSE PUBLISHERS
EUGENE, OREGON